Mel Bay Presents

# INTERNATIONAL FAVORITES FOR MANDOLIN

## BY JOE CARR

| Track Number | Page Number | Track Number | Page Number |
|---|---|---|---|
| 1. All Through The Night | 2 | 15. La Marseillaise | 18 |
| 2. America the Beautiful. | 3 | 16. Tá Mo Chleamhnas A Dhéanamh | 19 |
| 3. Aloha Oe | 4 | 17 There's No Place Like Home. | 20 |
| 4. Czardas | 6 | 18. Kum Ba Yah | 21 |
| 5. Arirang | 7 | 19. O Canada | 22 |
| 6. Battle Hymn of the Republic. | 8 | 20. Nací En El Cumbre | 23 |
| 7. Feng Yang | 9 | 21. My Old Kentucky Home | 24 |
| 8. Ack Värmeland Du Sköna | 10 | 22 Herr Roloff's Farewell | 26 |
| 9. Sur le Pont d'Avignon | 11 | 23. Tarantella | 28 |
| 10. Du, Du liegst mir am Herzen | 12 | 24. Volga Boatman | 29 |
| 11. Greensleeves | 13 | 25. Waltzing Matilda | 30 |
| 12. Hava Nagila | 14 | 26. Riu Chiu | 31 |
| 13. Las Mañanitas | 16 | 27. Sakura | 31 |
| 14. Planxty Irwin | 17 | 28. The U. S. National Anthem | 32 |

Lead instruments on the CD include mandolin, octave mandolin and Irish tenor banjo and are tuned GDAE

Cover photo courtesy of Michael Kelly™ Guitar Company, www.michaelkellyguitars.com

1 2 3 4 5 6 7 8 9 0

© 2004 BY MEL BAY PUBLICATIONS, INC., PACIFIC, MO 63069.
ALL RIGHTS RESERVED. INTERNATIONAL COPYRIGHT SECURED. B.M.I. MADE AND PRINTED IN U.S.A.
No part of this publication may be reproduced in whole or in part, or stored in a retrieval system, or transmitted in any form
or by any means, electronic, mechanical, photocopy, recording, or otherwise, without written permission of the publisher.

**Visit us on the Web at www.melbay.com — E-mail us at email@melbay.com**

# All Through The Night

Wales

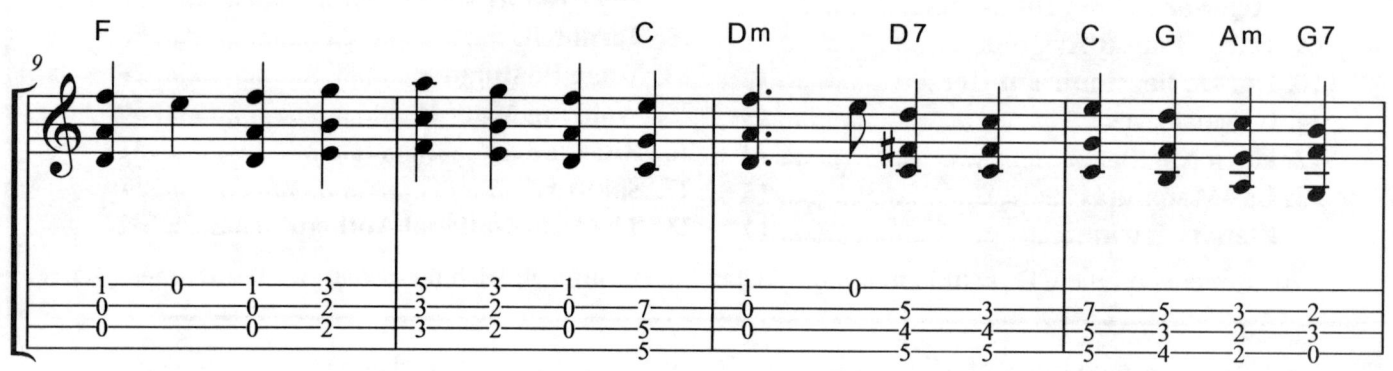

# America, The Beautiful

United States

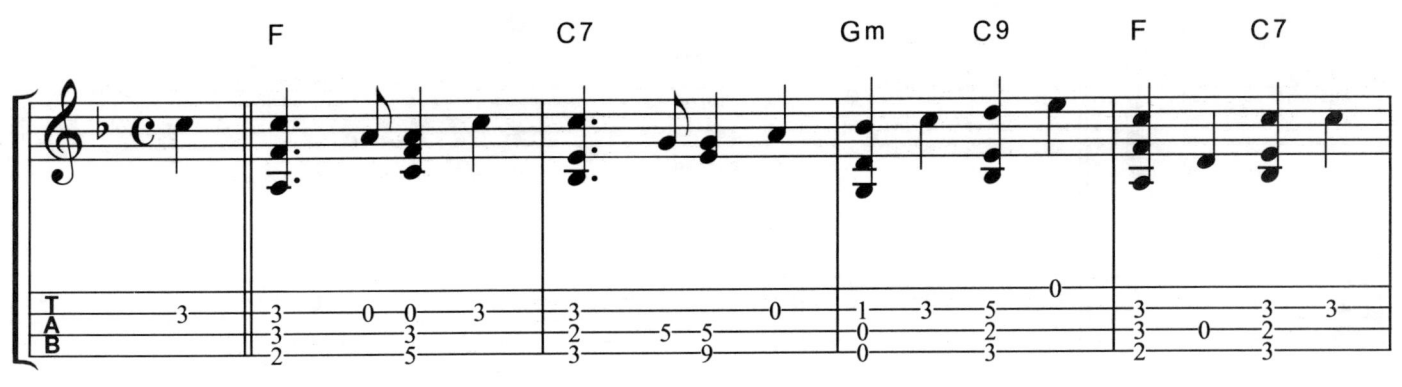
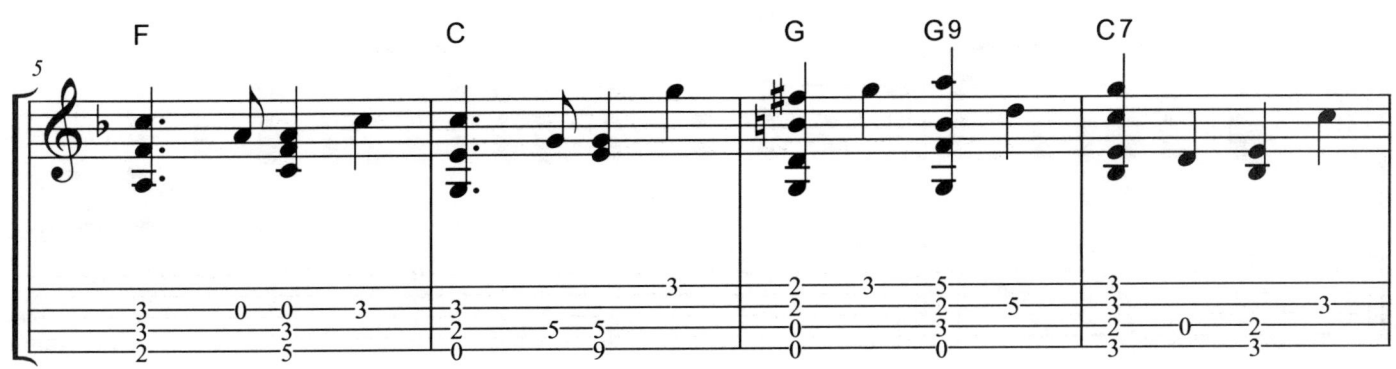
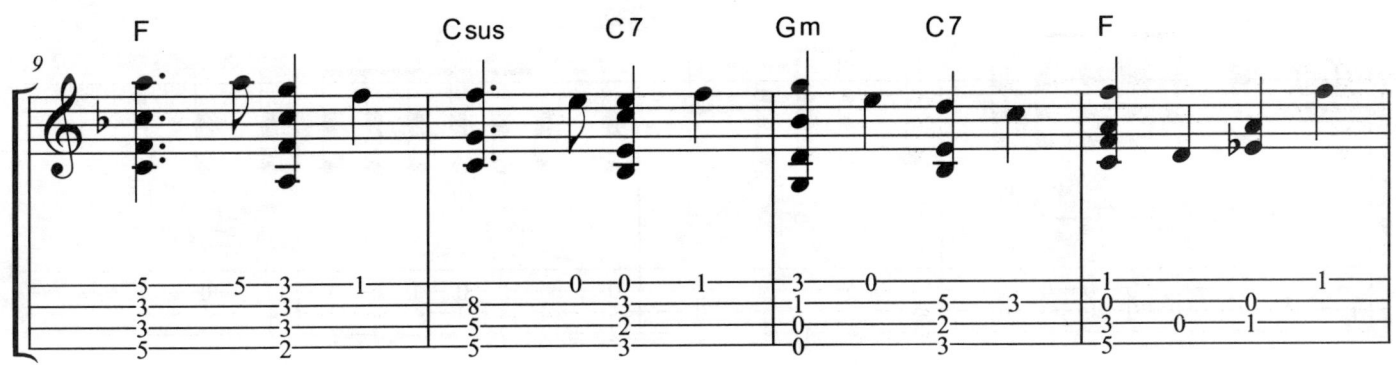

# Aloha Oe

Hawaii

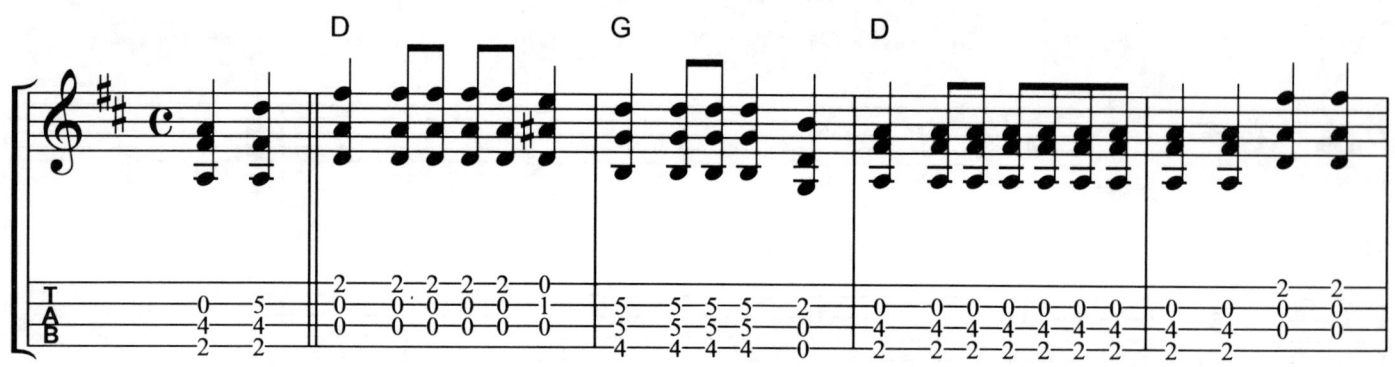
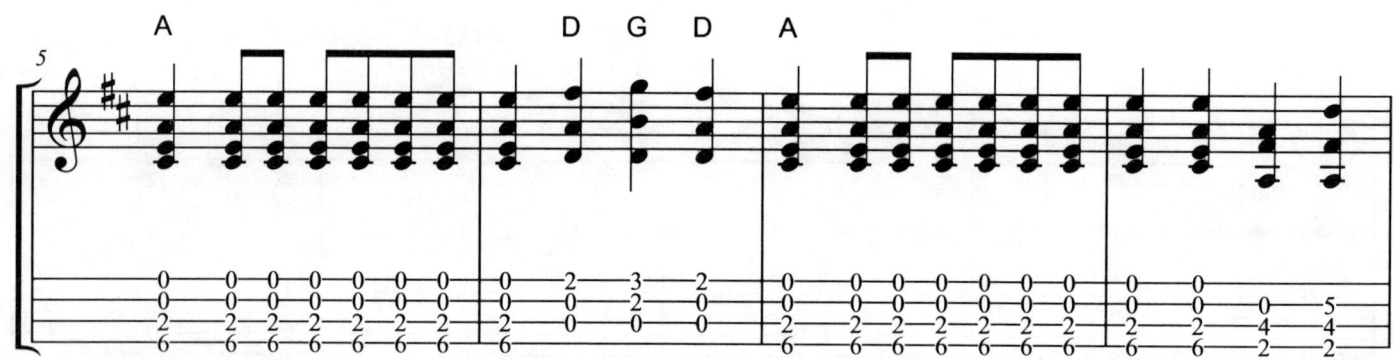
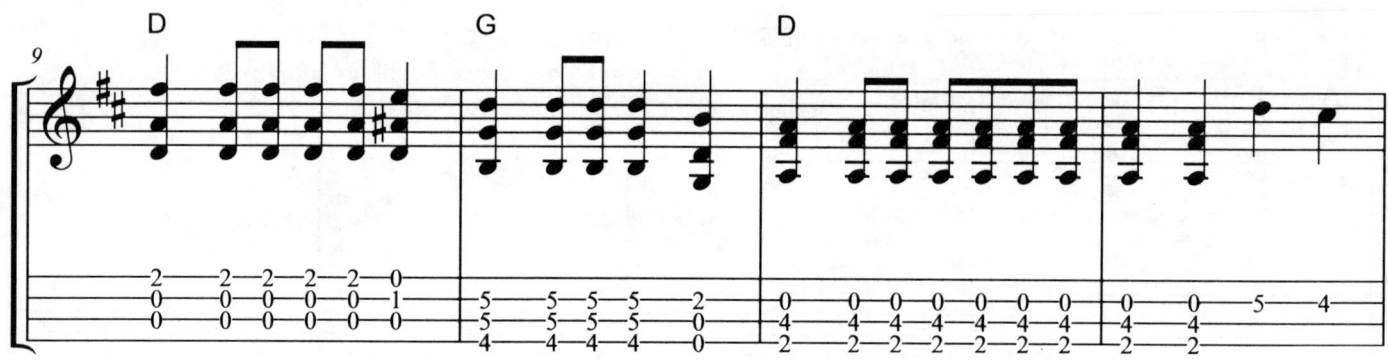

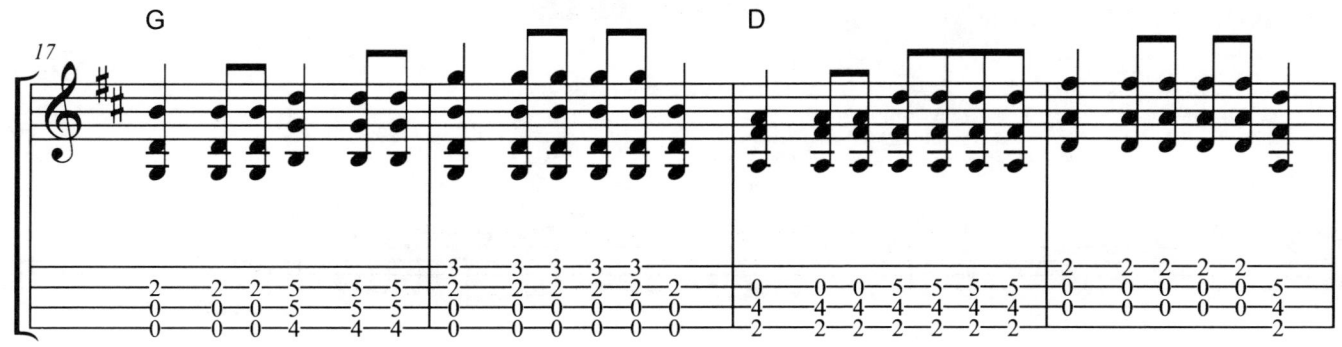
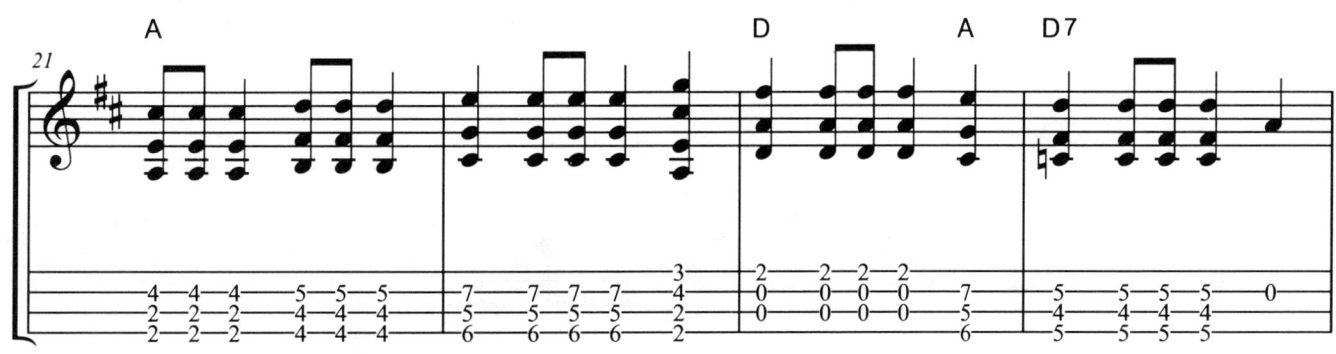
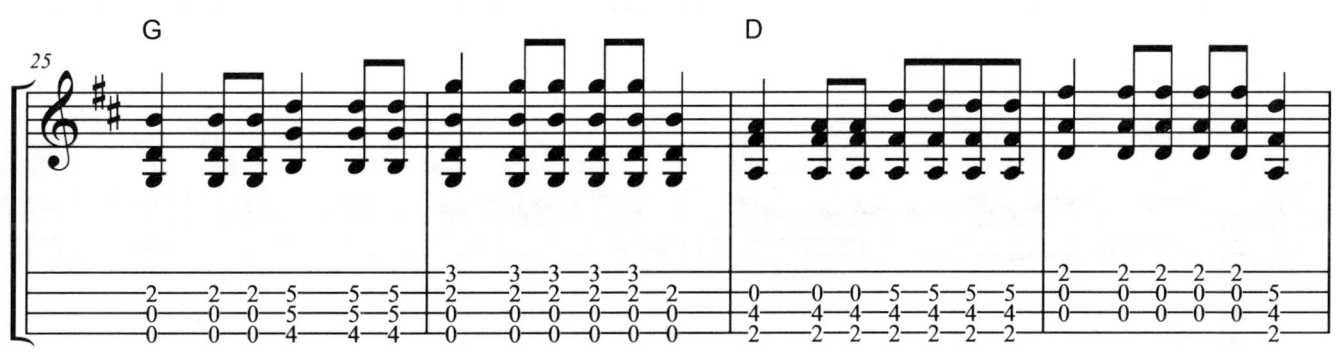
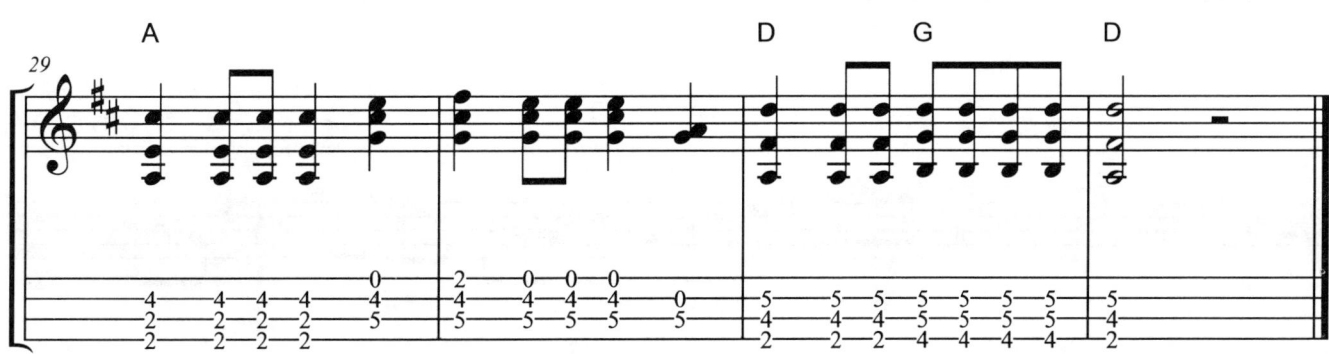

# Czardas

**Moravia**

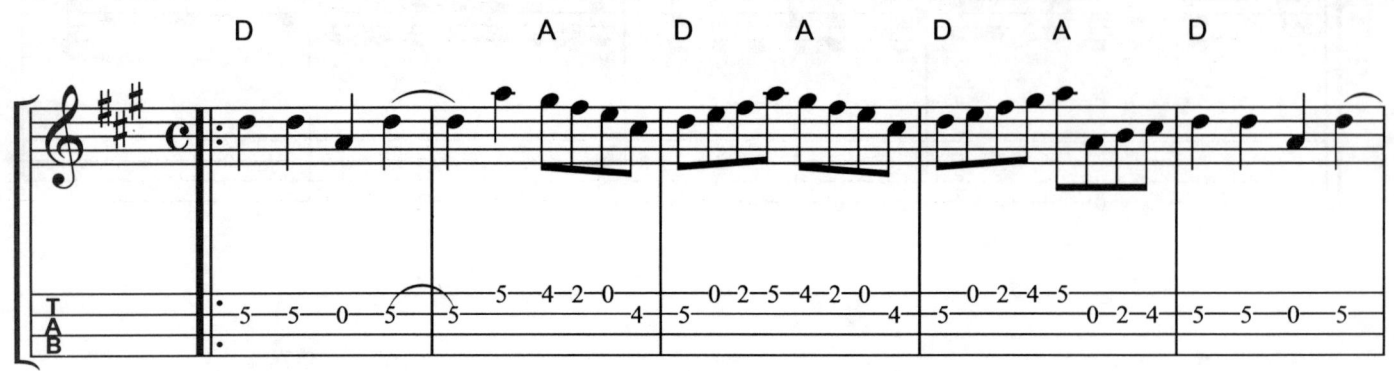
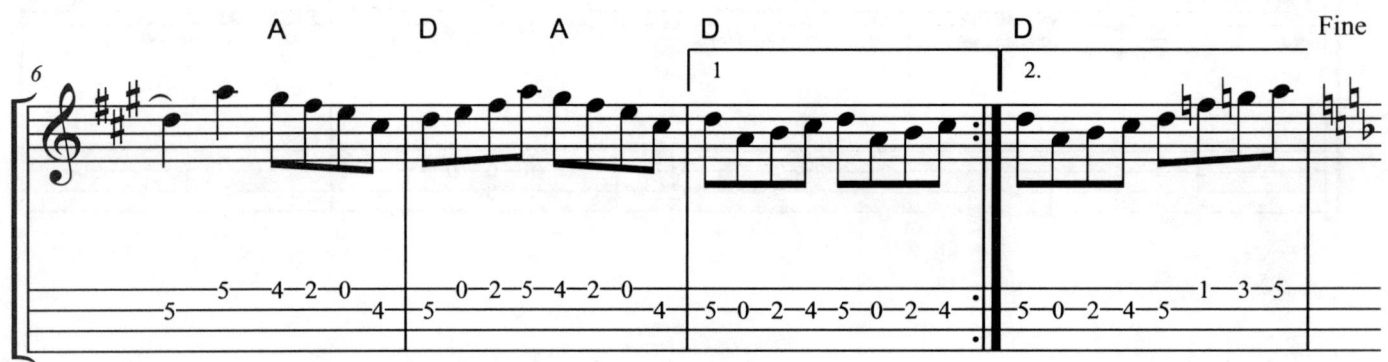
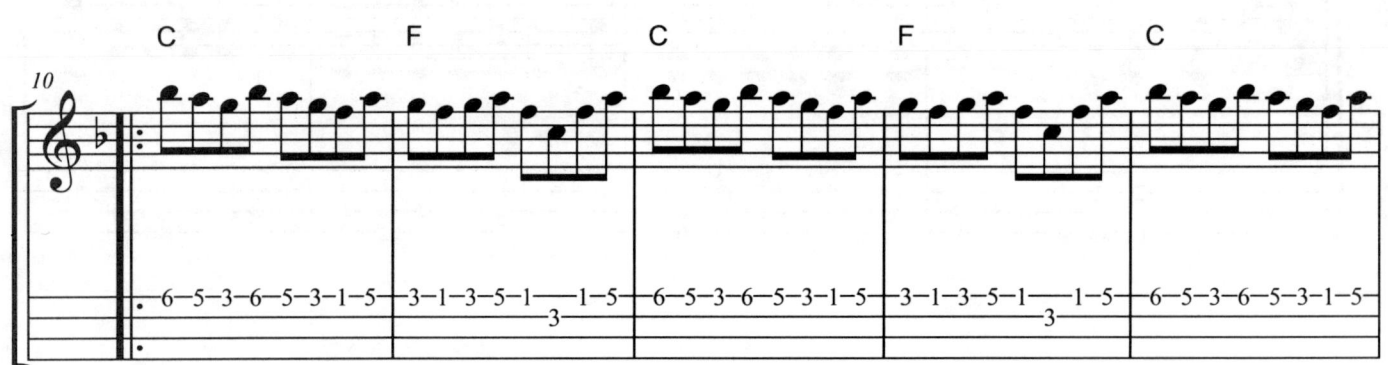
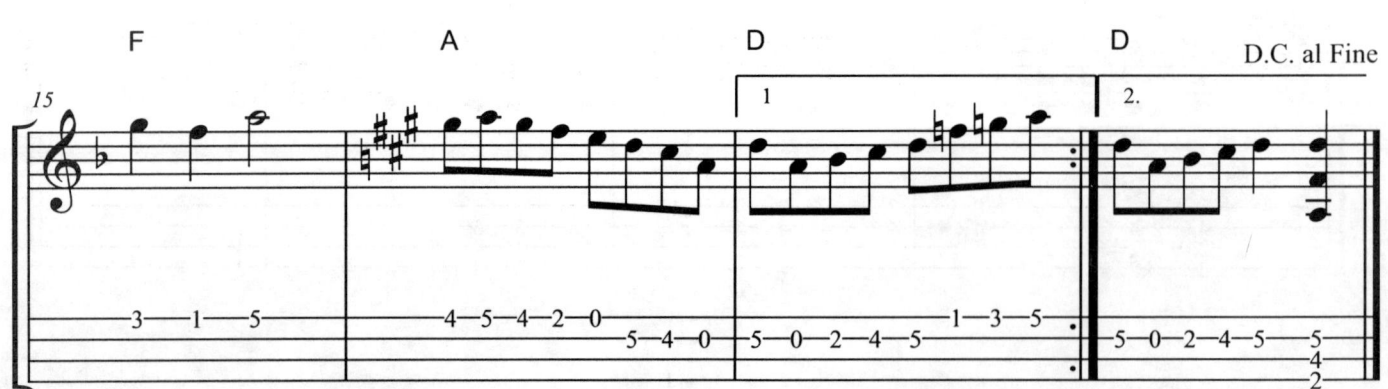

# Arirang

**Korea**

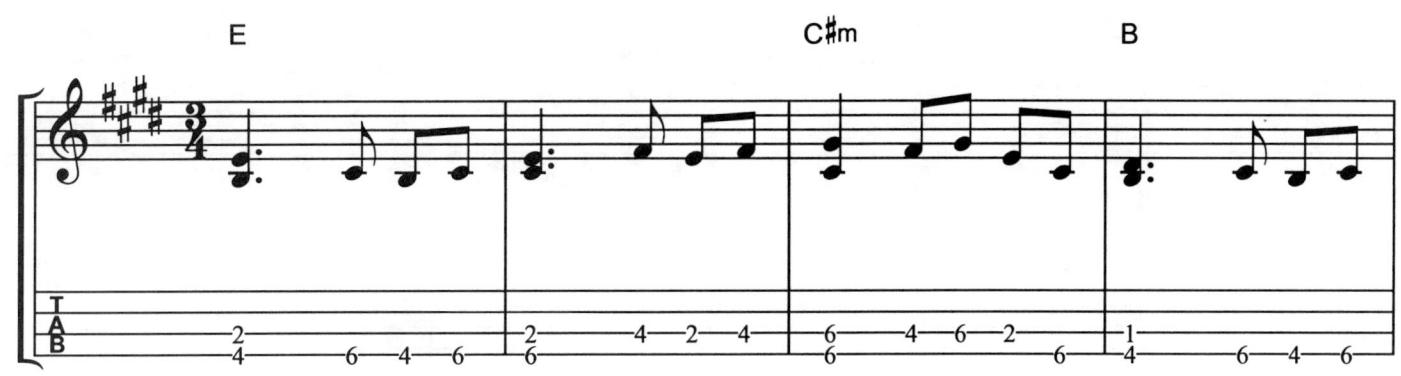

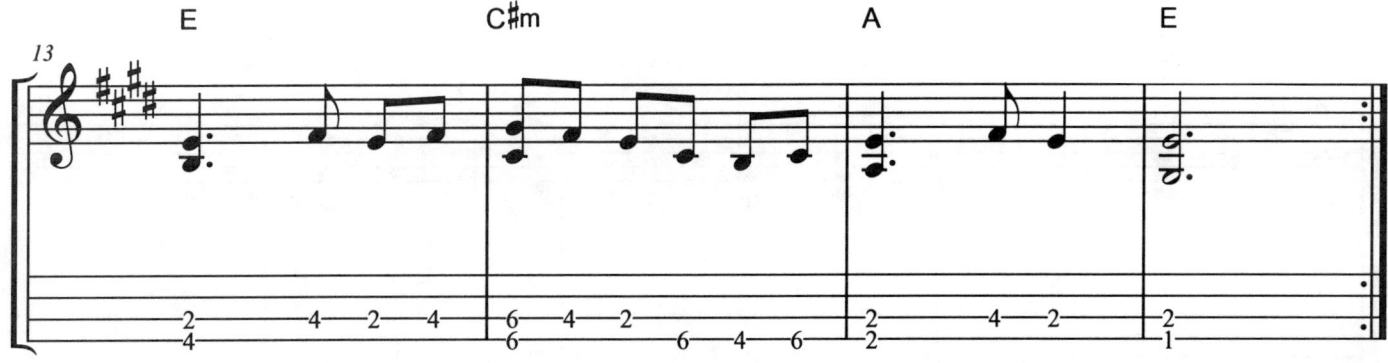

# Battle Hymn of the Republic

United States

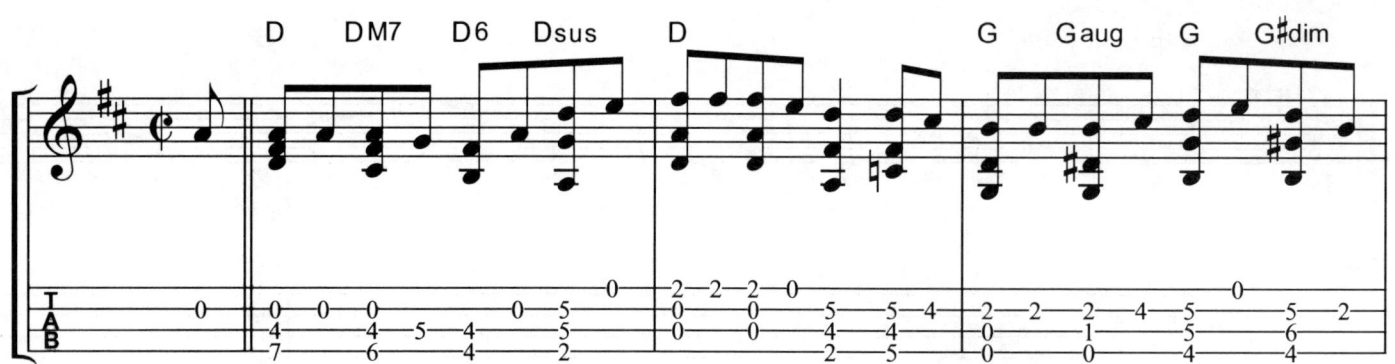
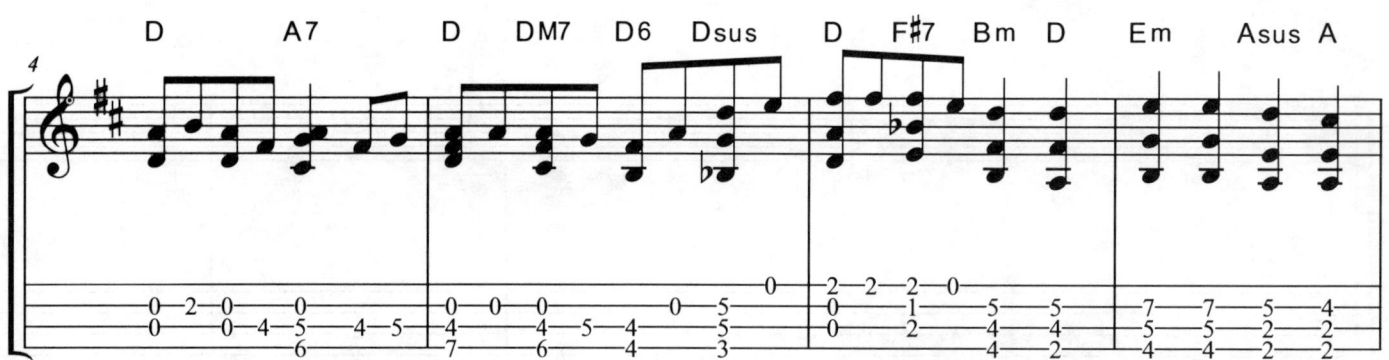
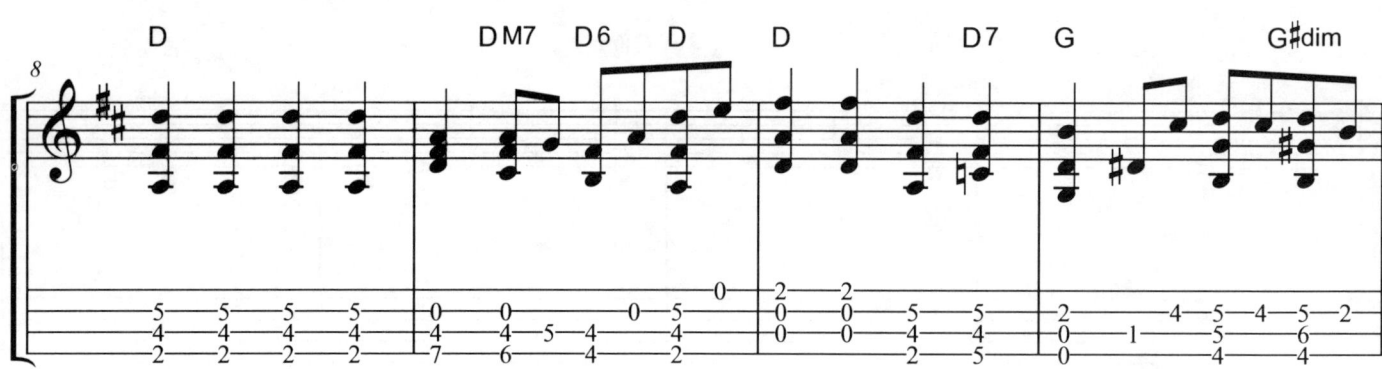
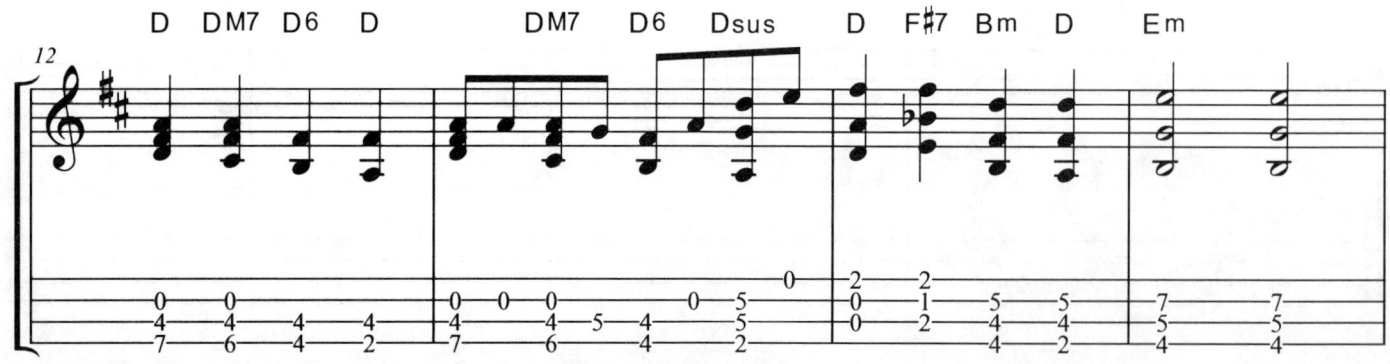

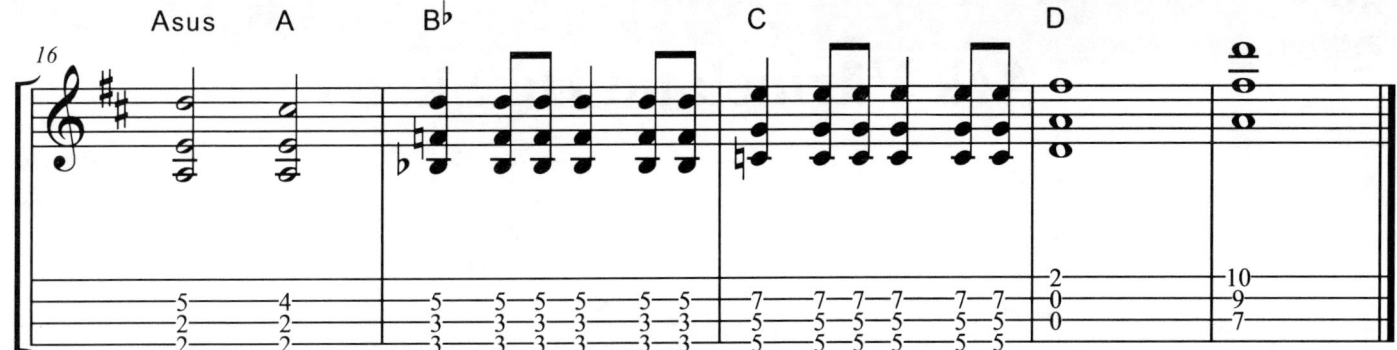

## Feng Yang

China

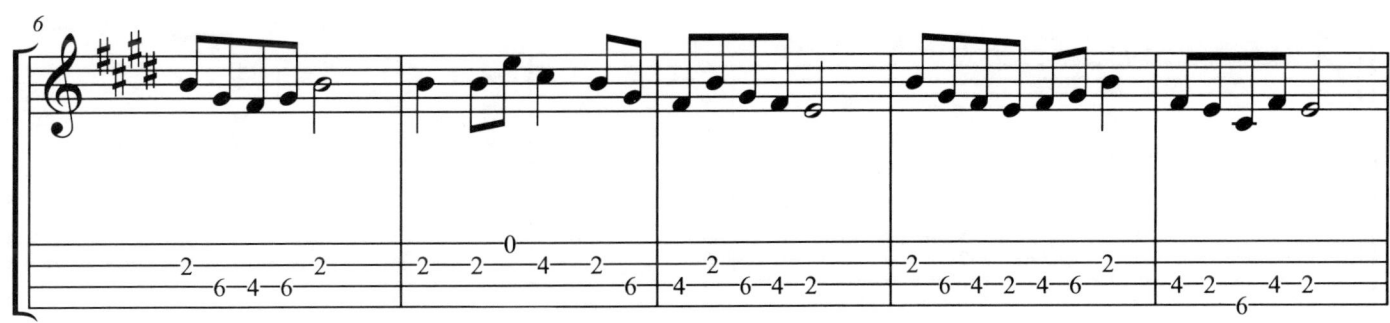

# Ack Värmeland Du Sköna

Sweden

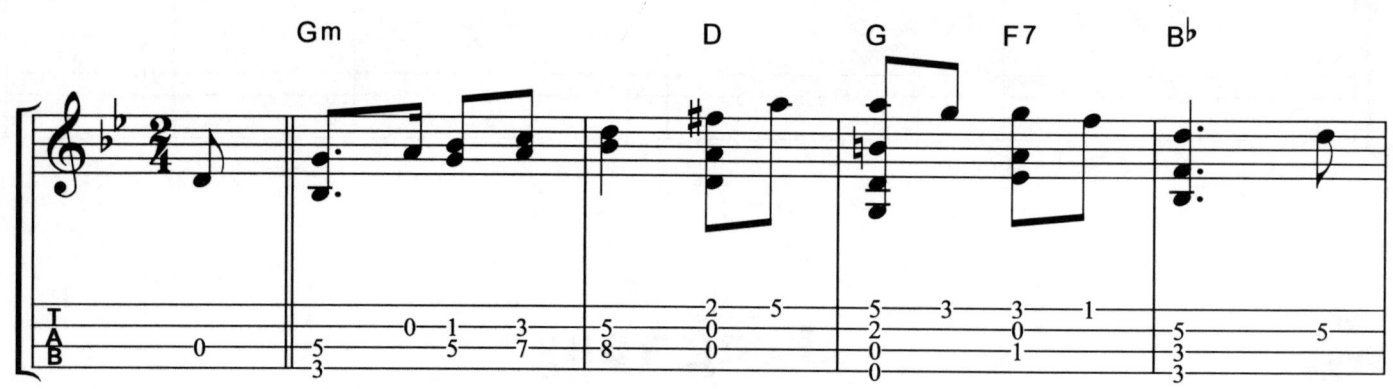
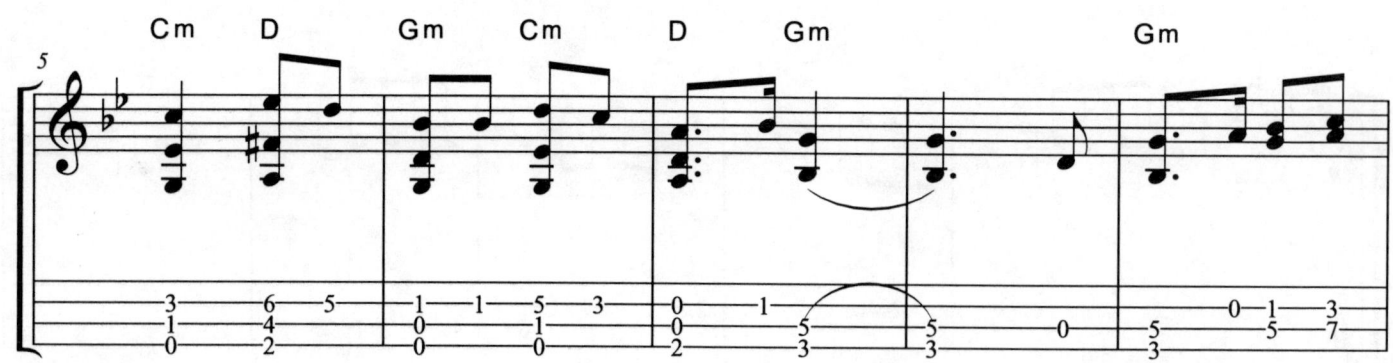
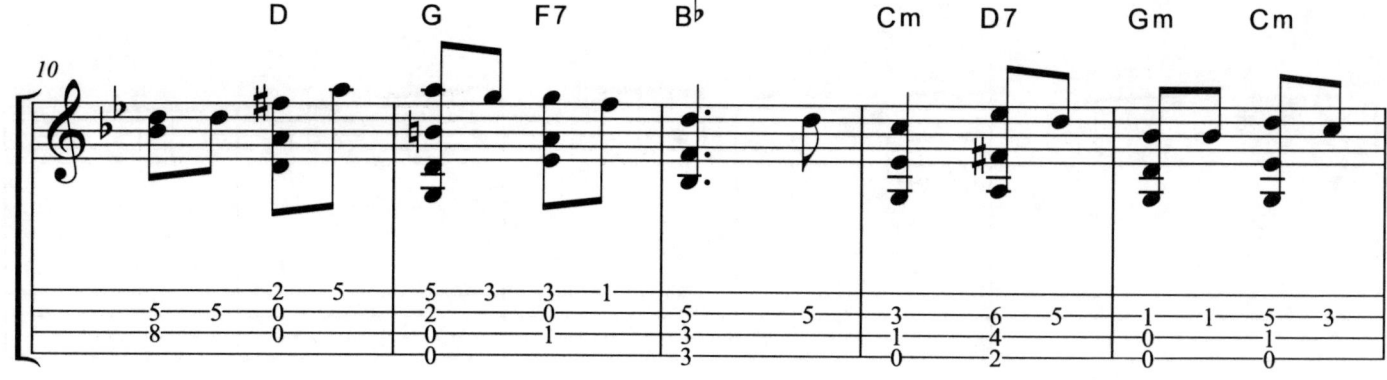
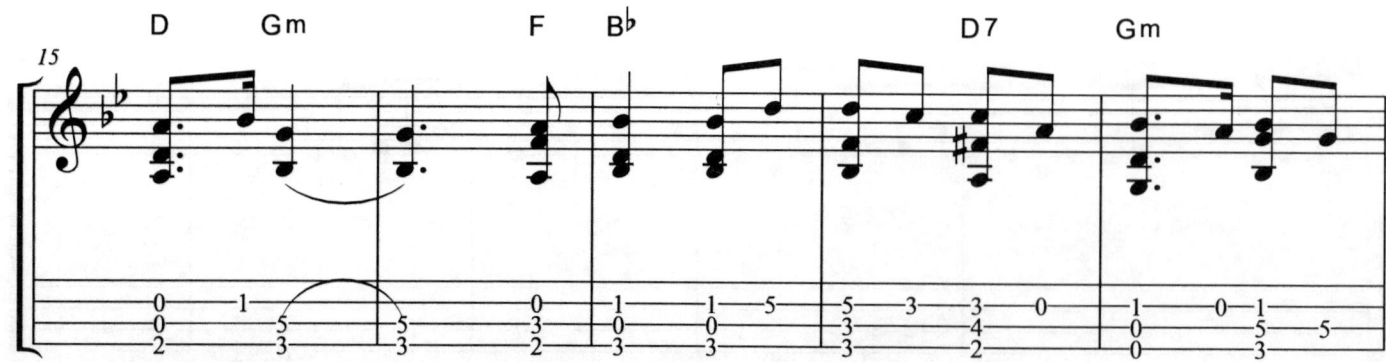

## Sur le Pont d'Avignon

France

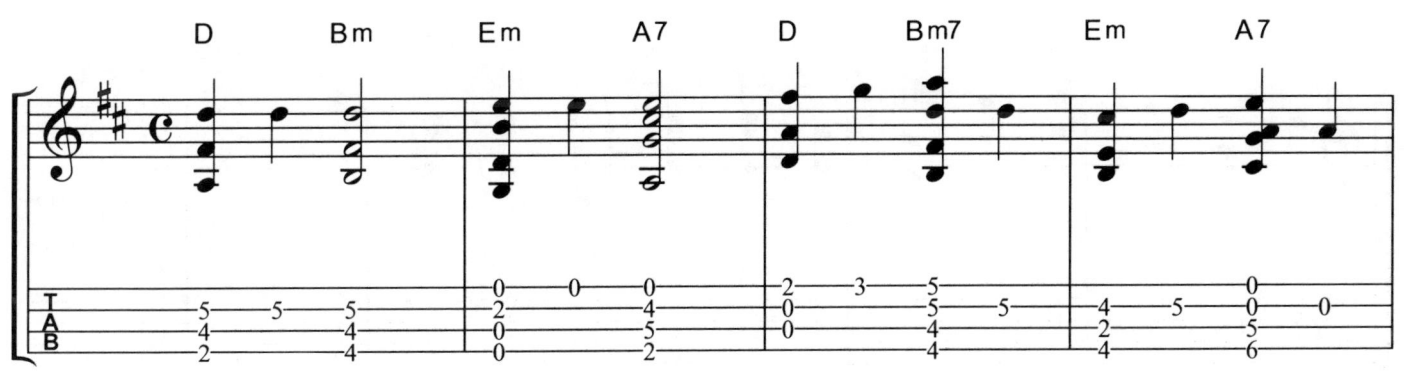

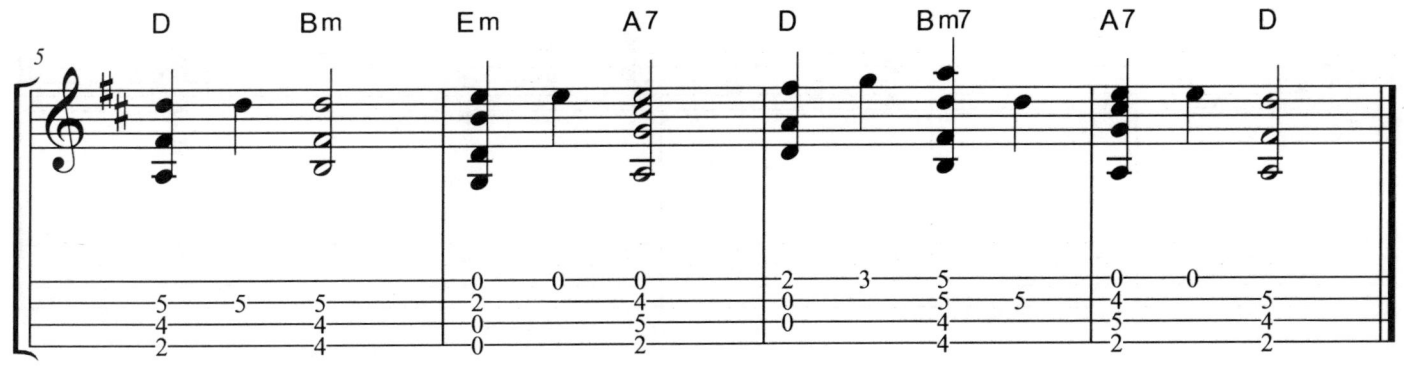

# Du, du liegst mir am Herzen

Germany

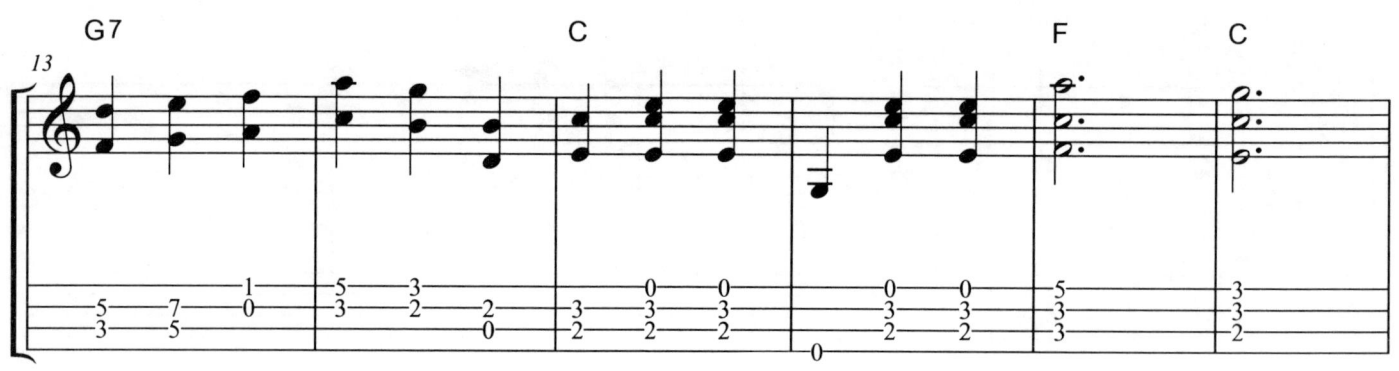
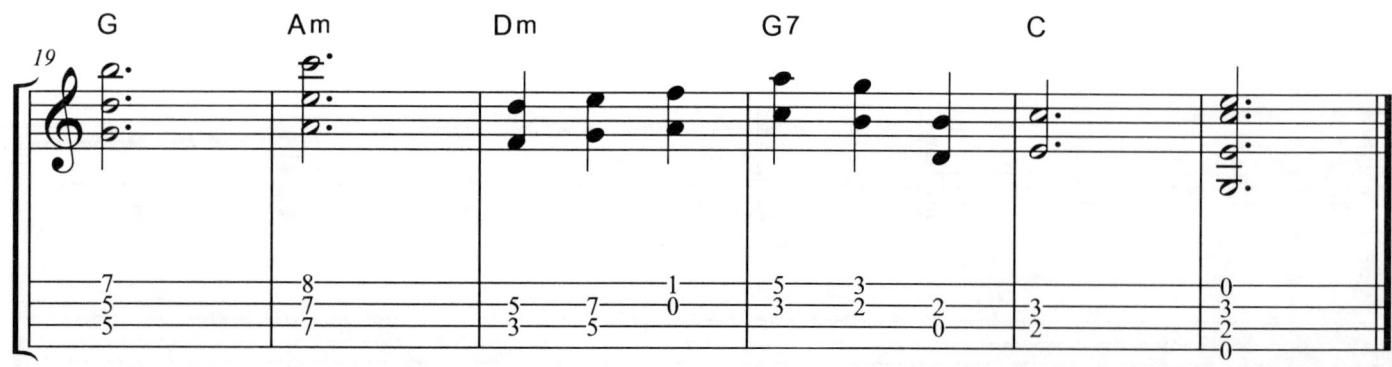

# Greensleeves

**England**

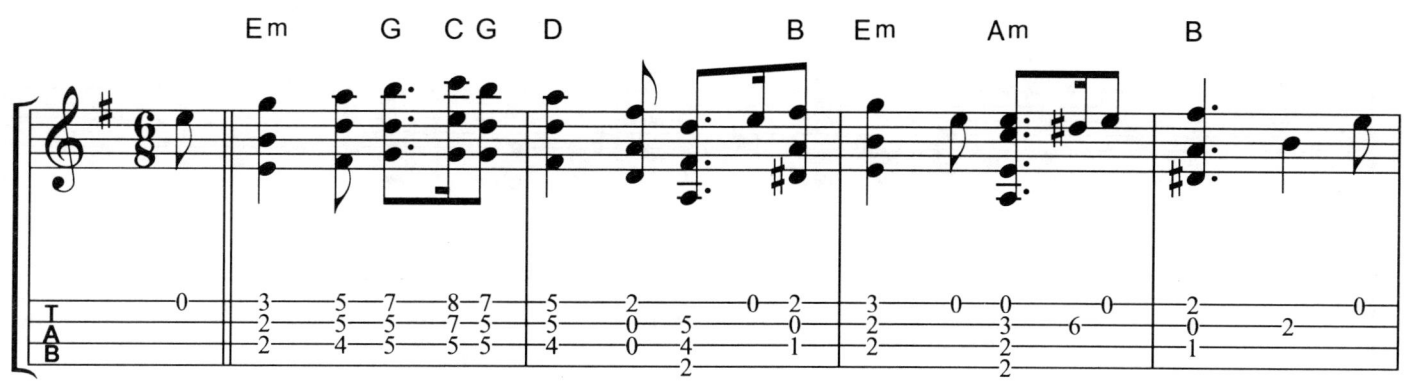
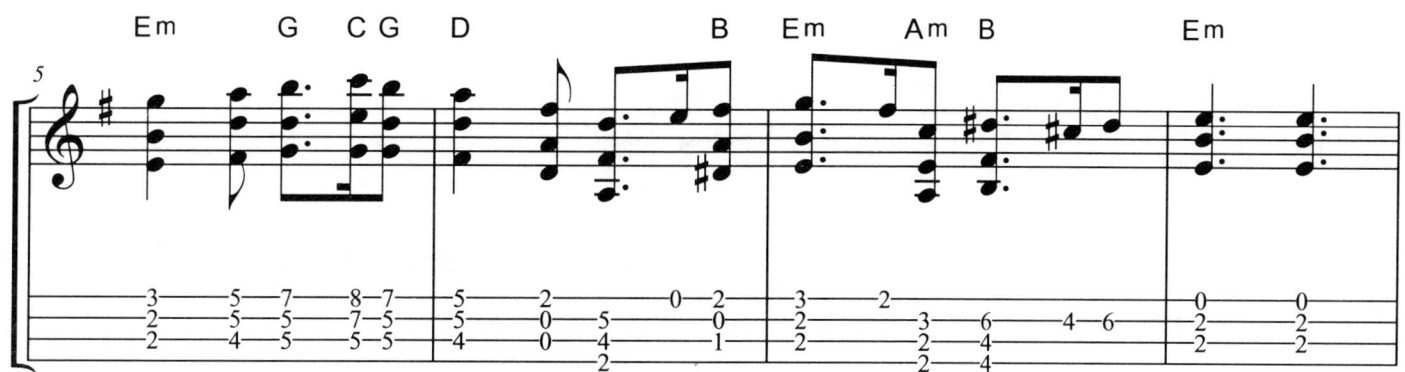
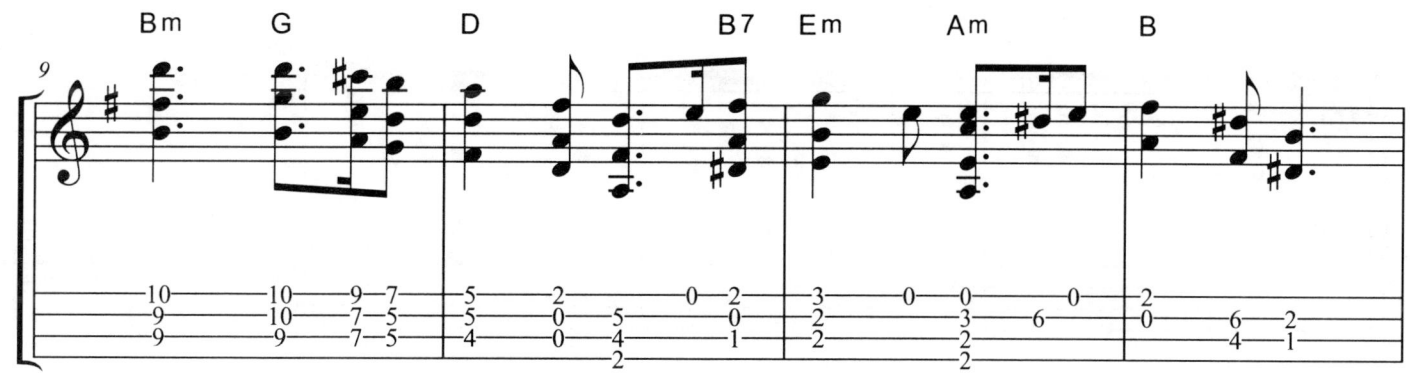
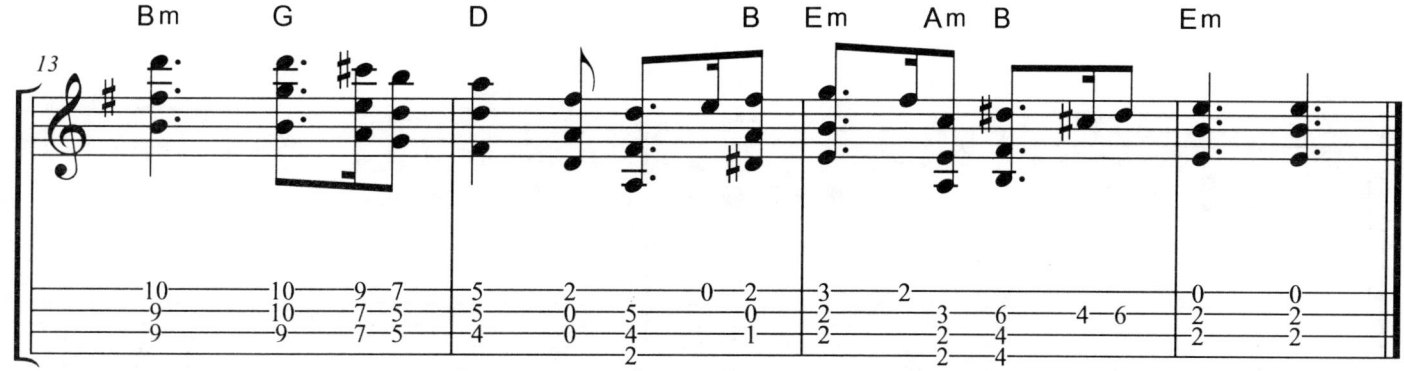

# Hava Nagila

Israel

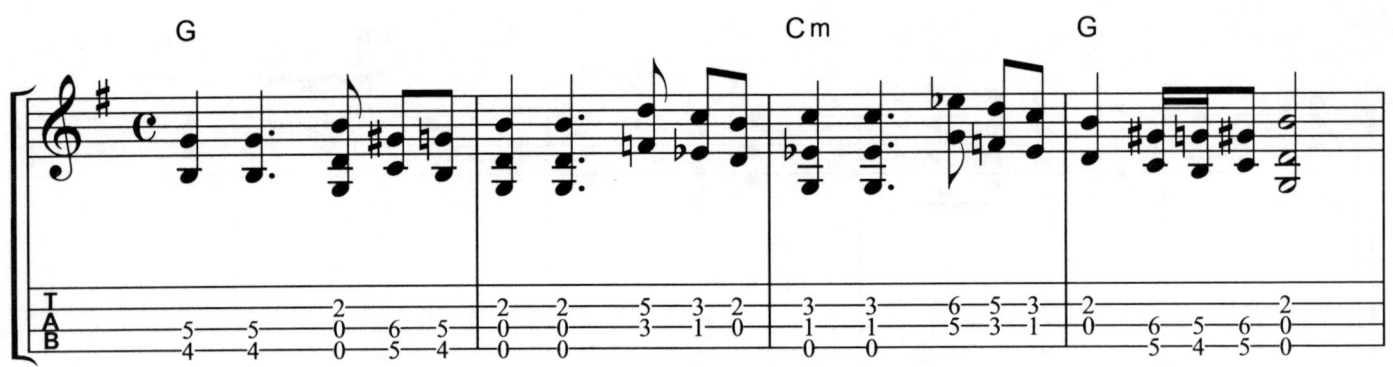
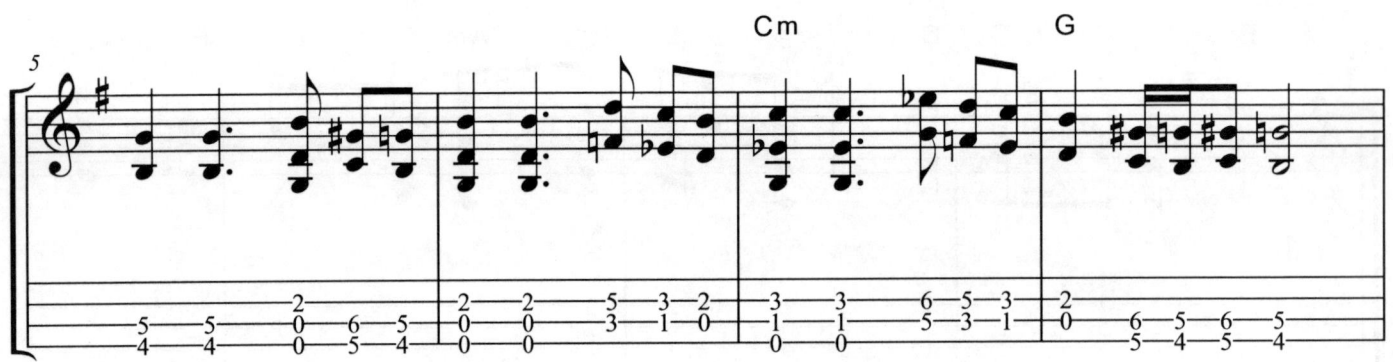

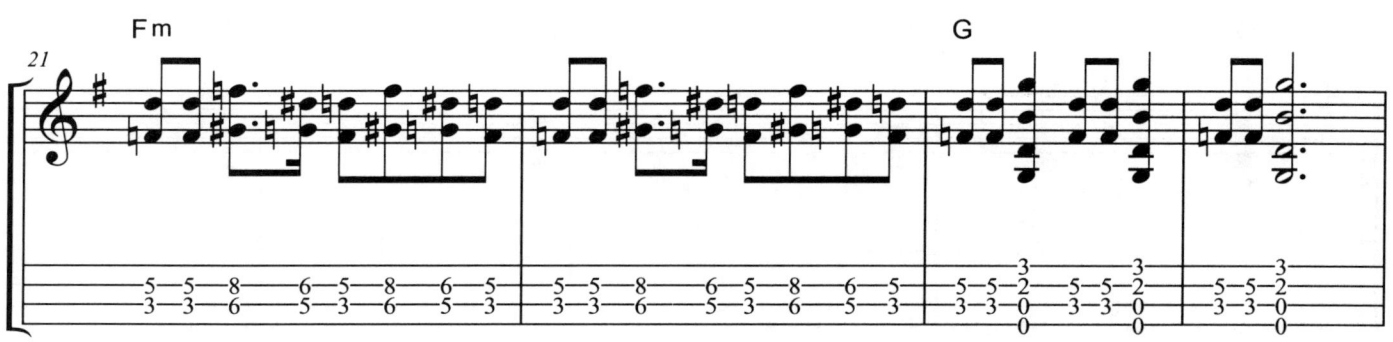

# Las Mañanitas

Mexico

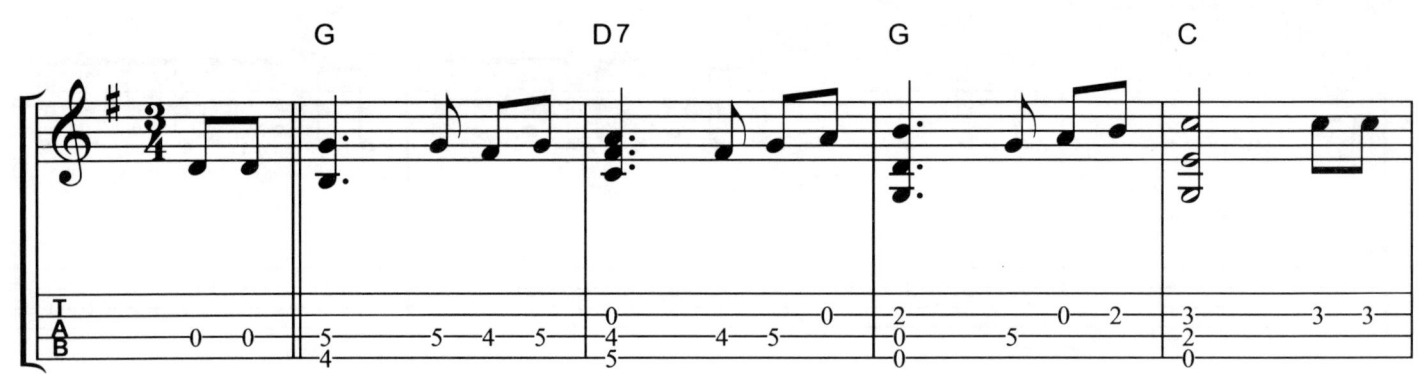

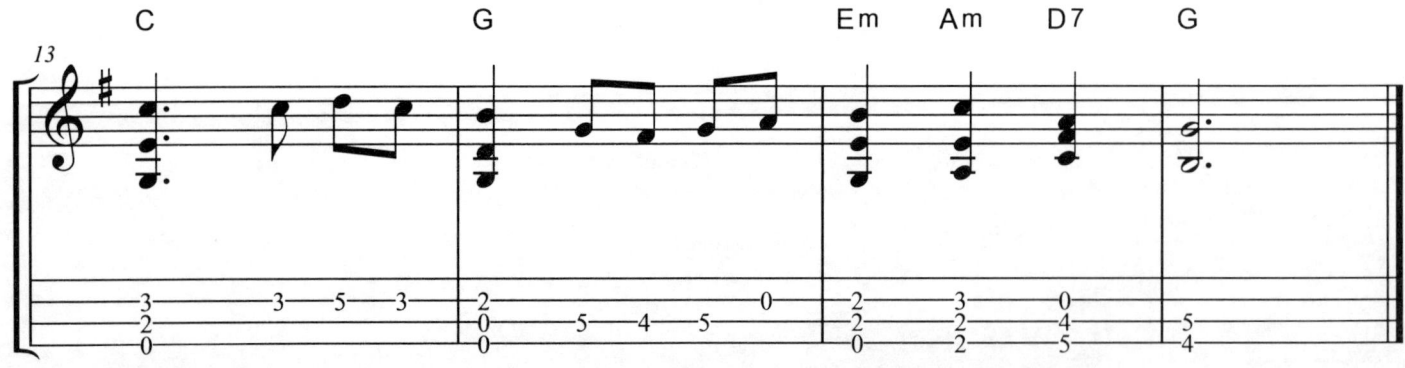

# Planxty Irwin

Ireland

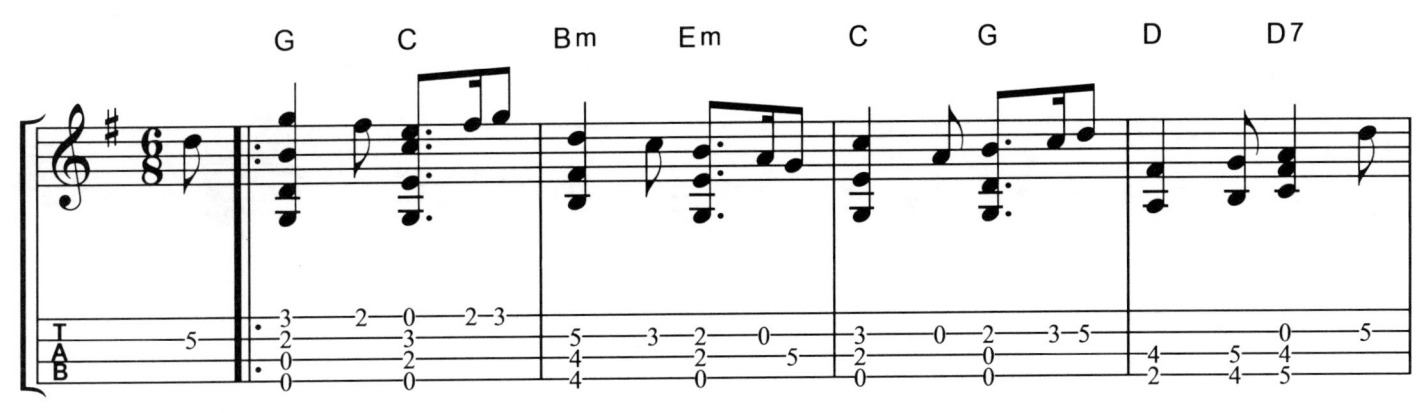
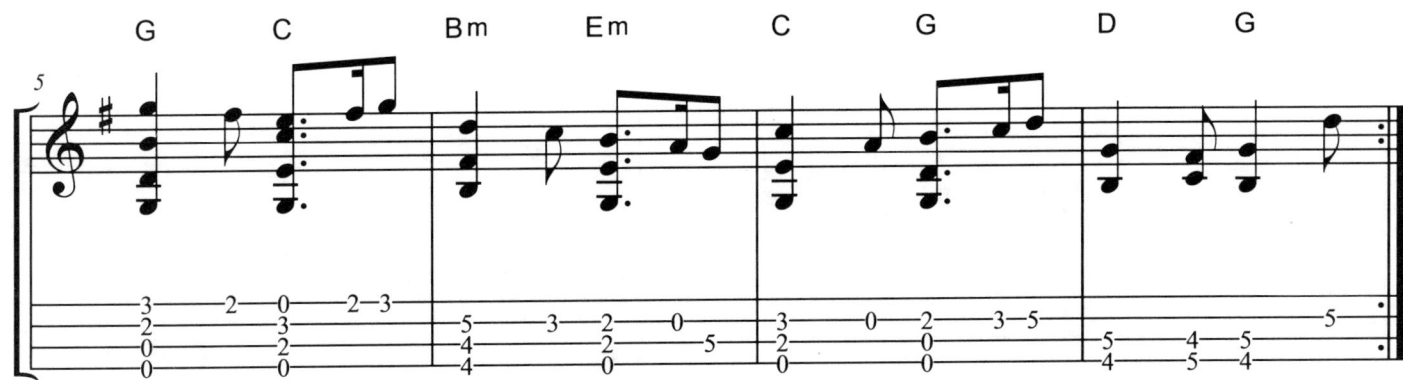
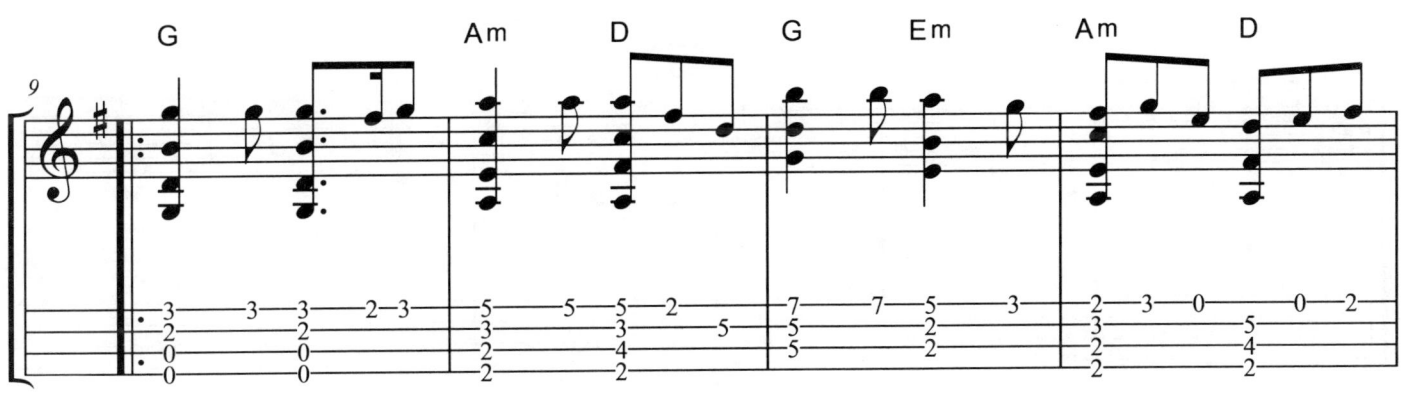
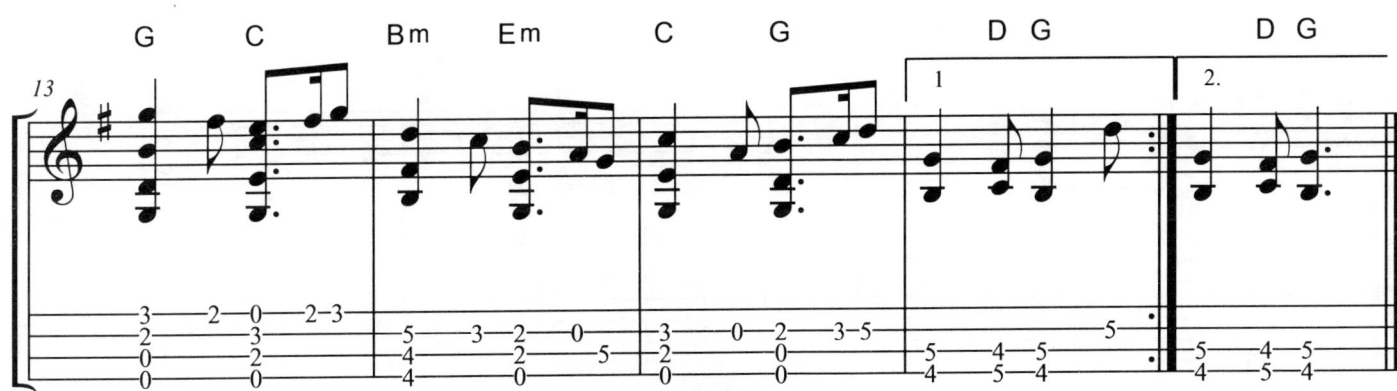

# La Marseillaise

France

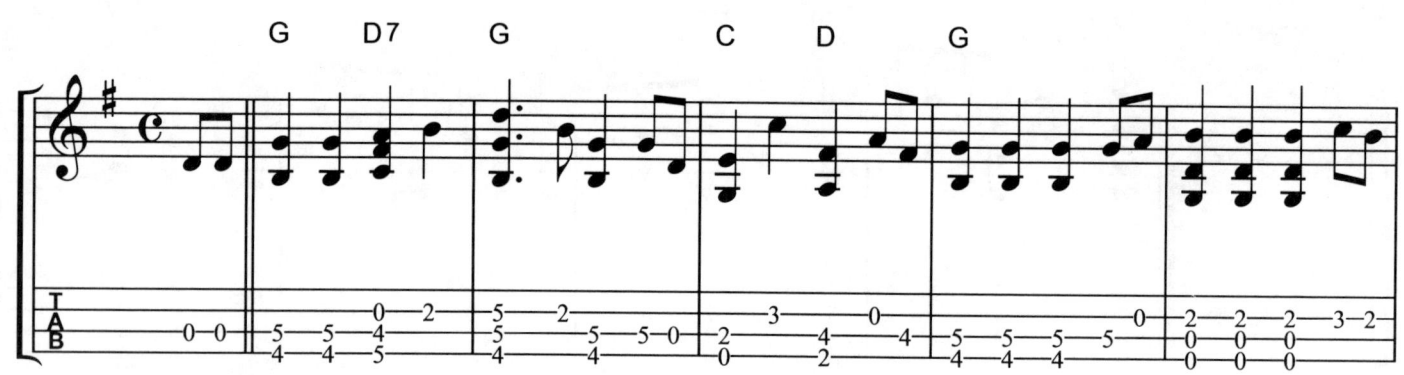
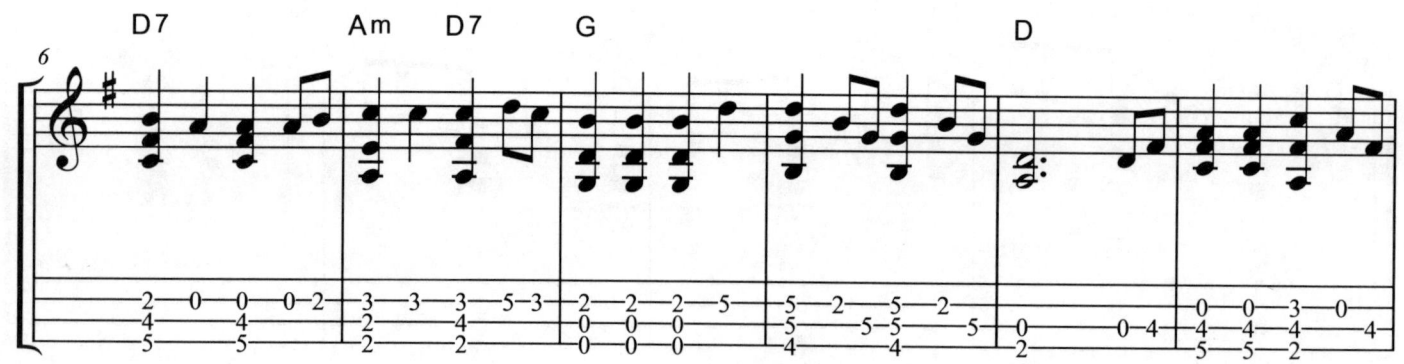
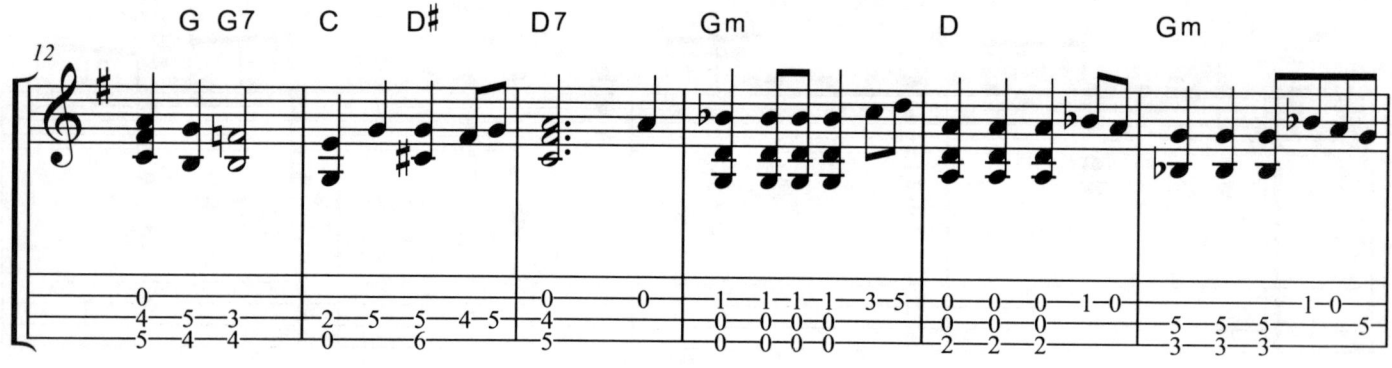
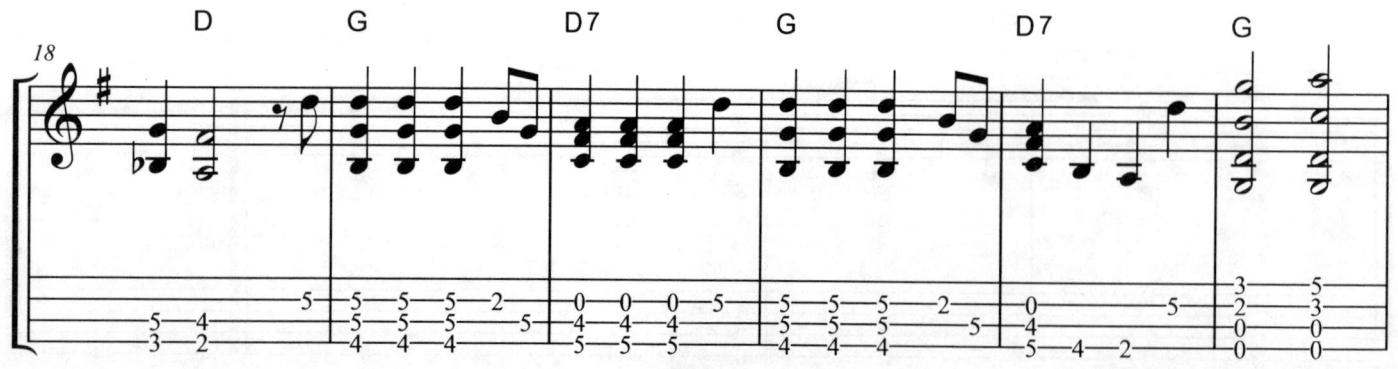

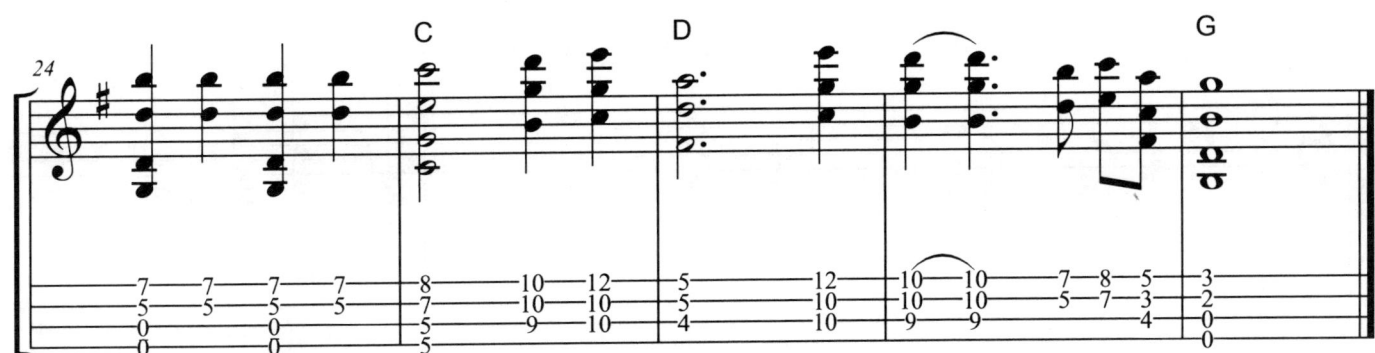

 ## Tá Mo Chleamhas A Dhéanamh

**Ireland - Gaelic**

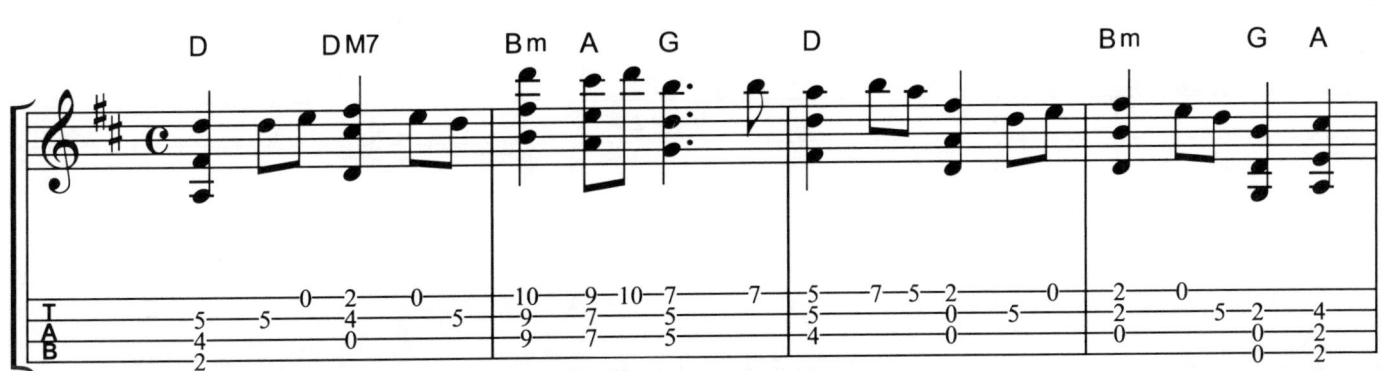

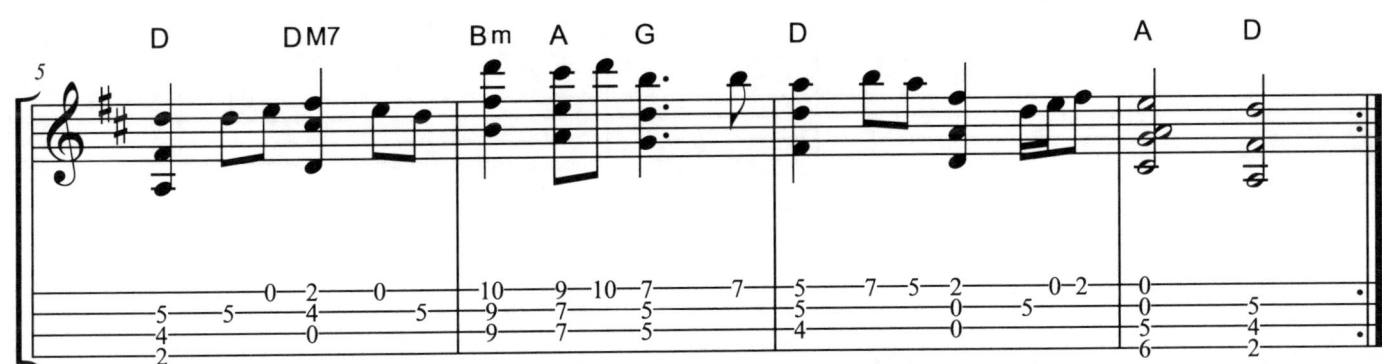

# There's No Place Like Home

United States

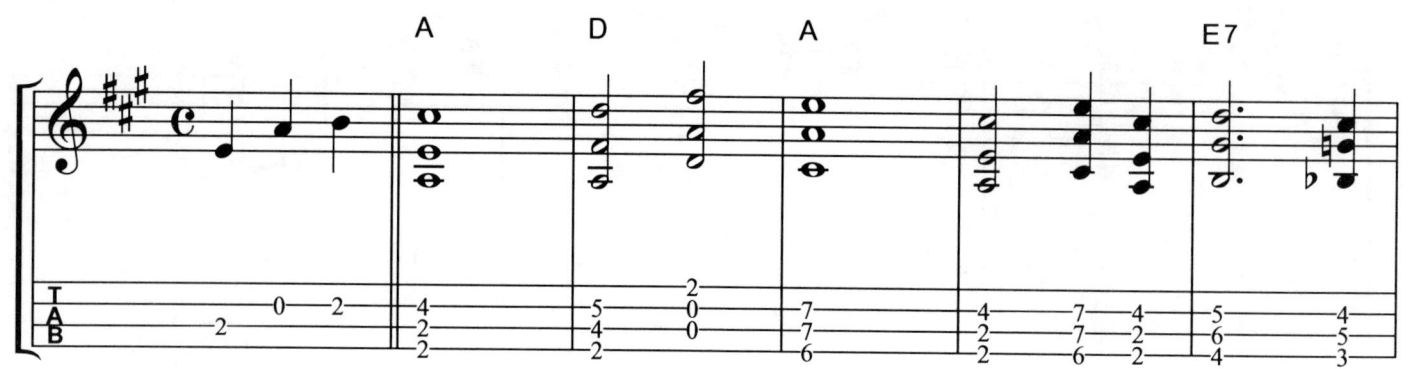

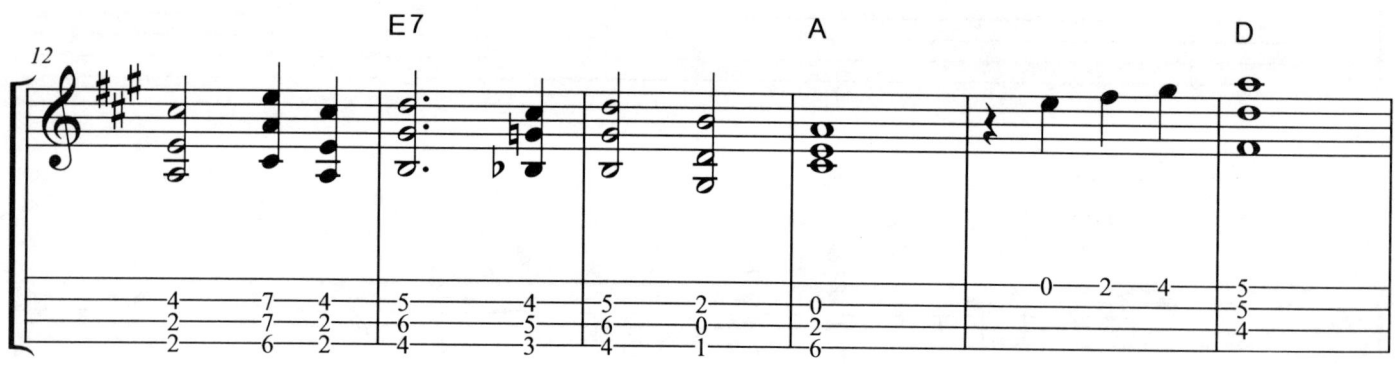

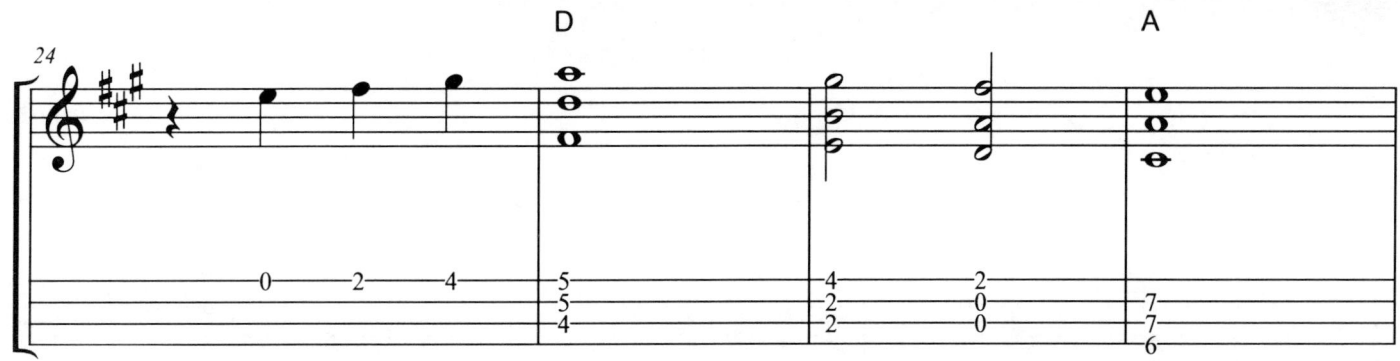

# Kum Ba Yah

**Africa**

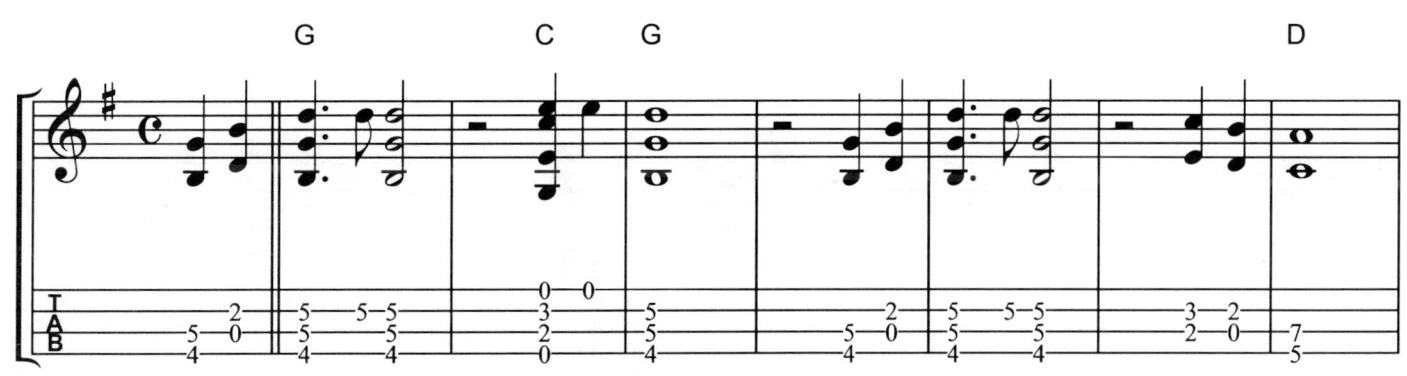

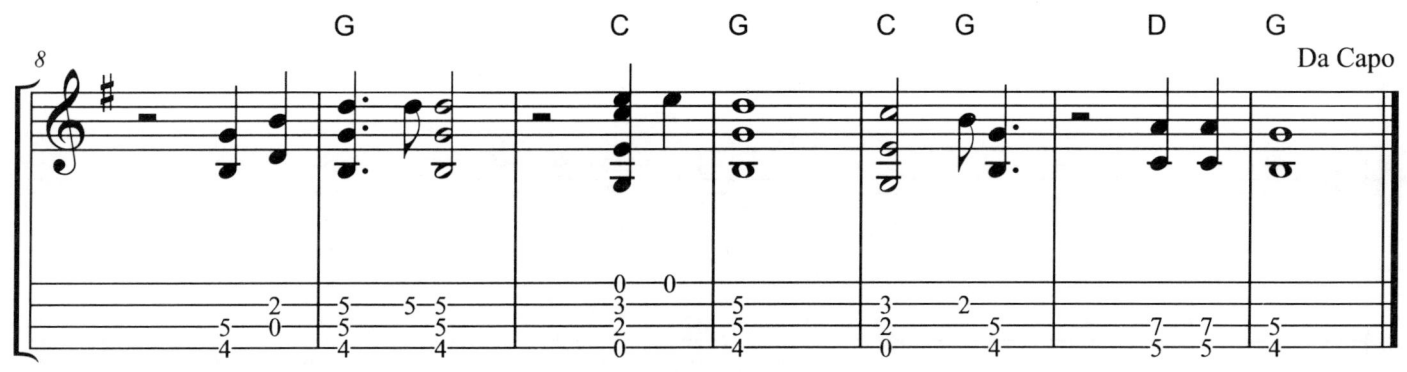

# O Canada

**Canada**

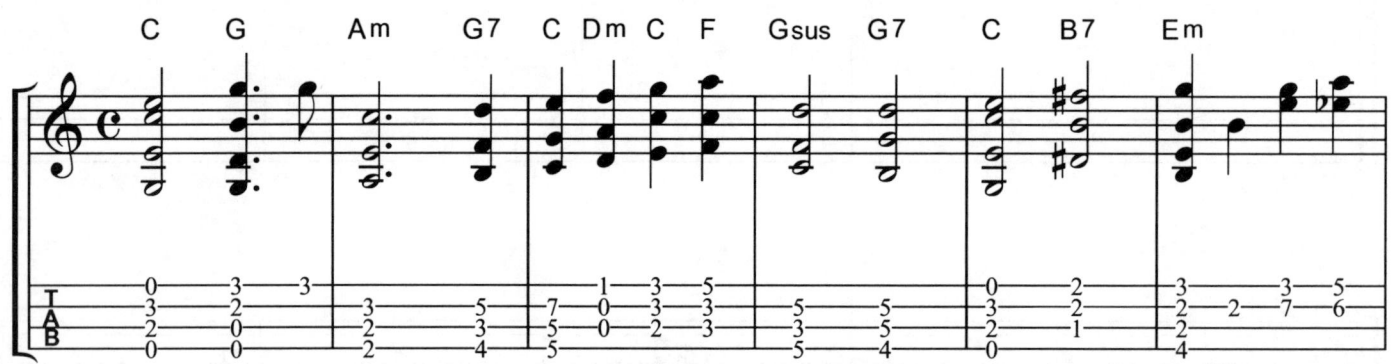
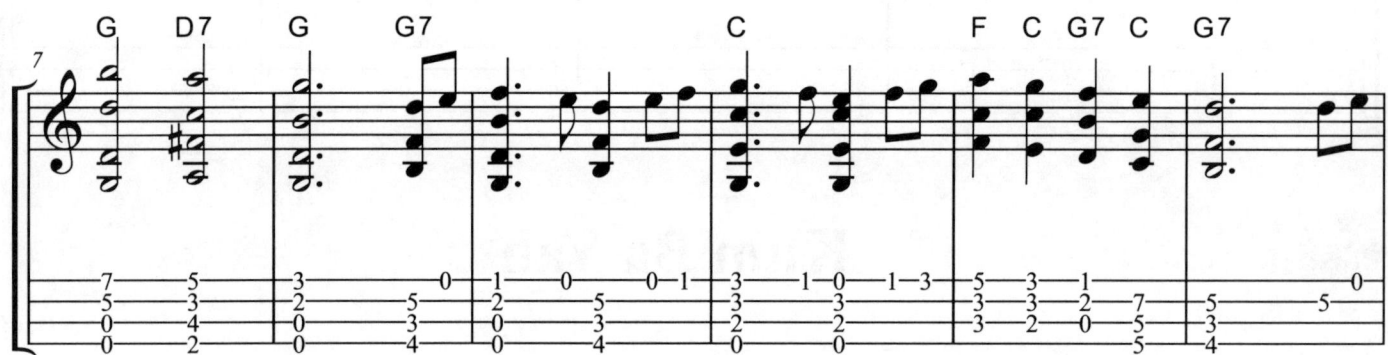
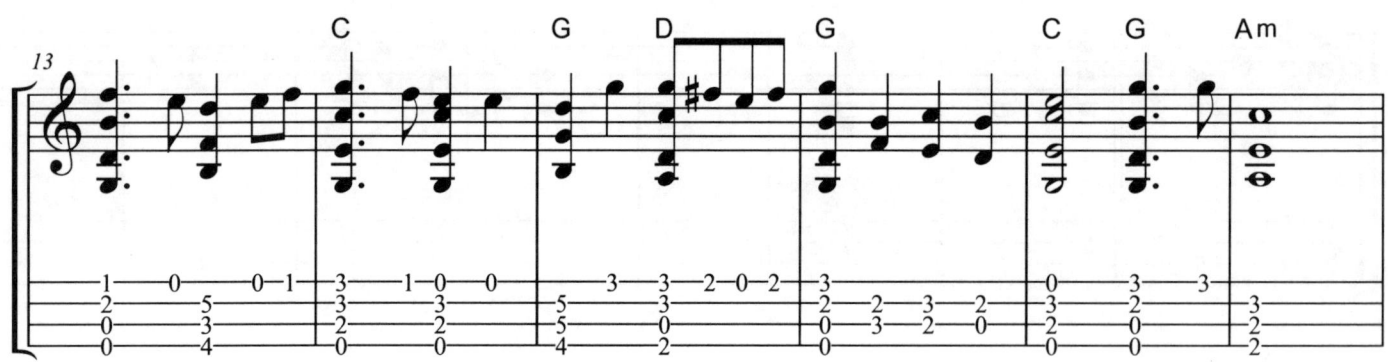

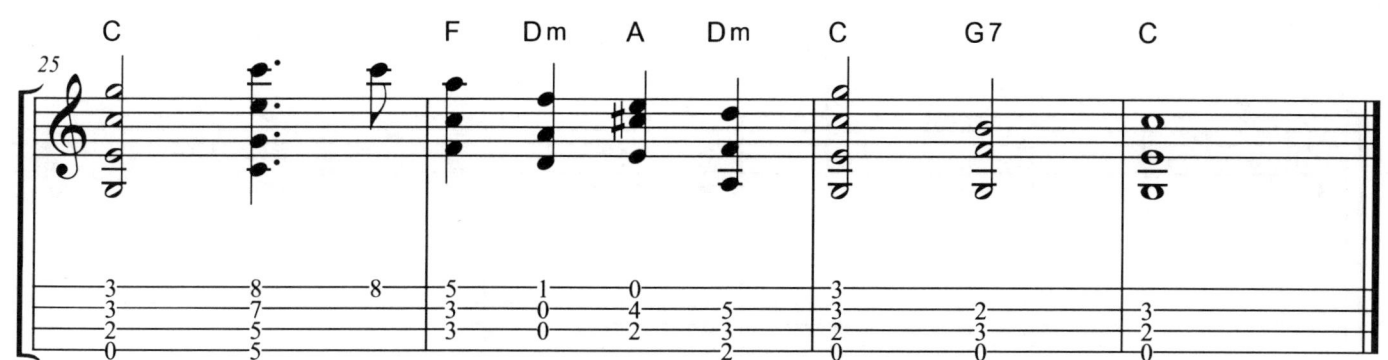

## Nací En La Cumbre

**Guatemala**

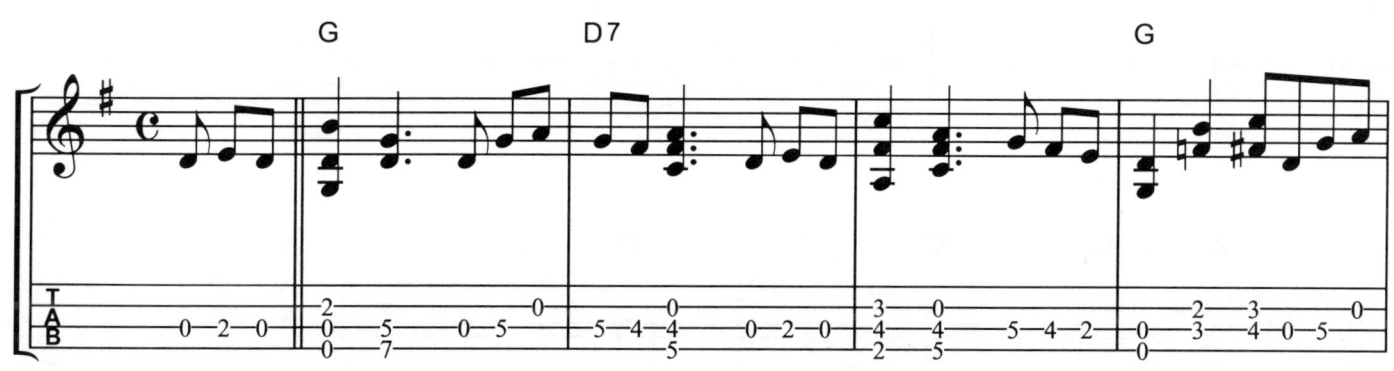

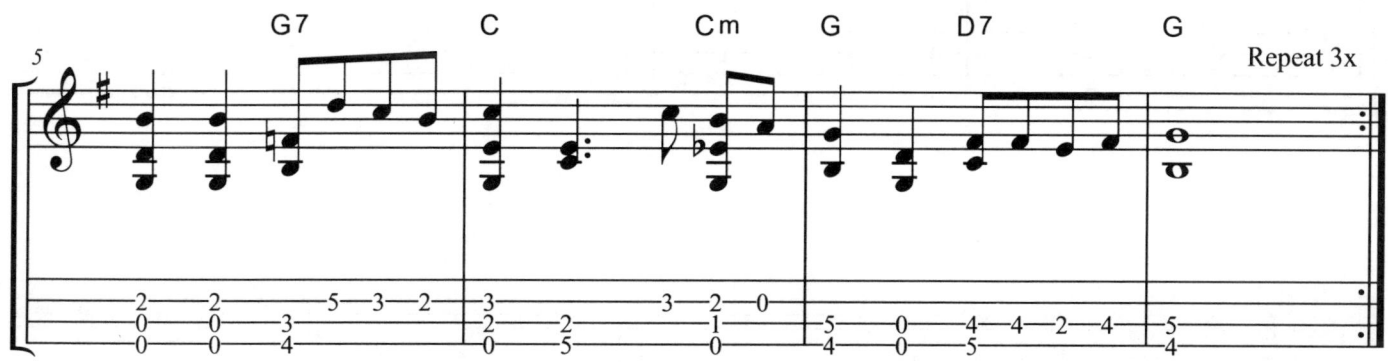

# My Old Kentucky Home

United States

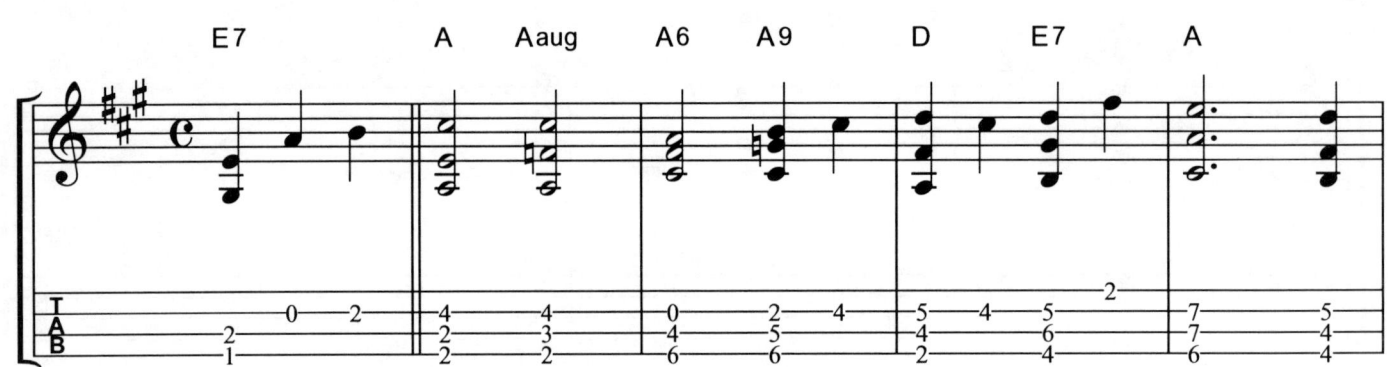
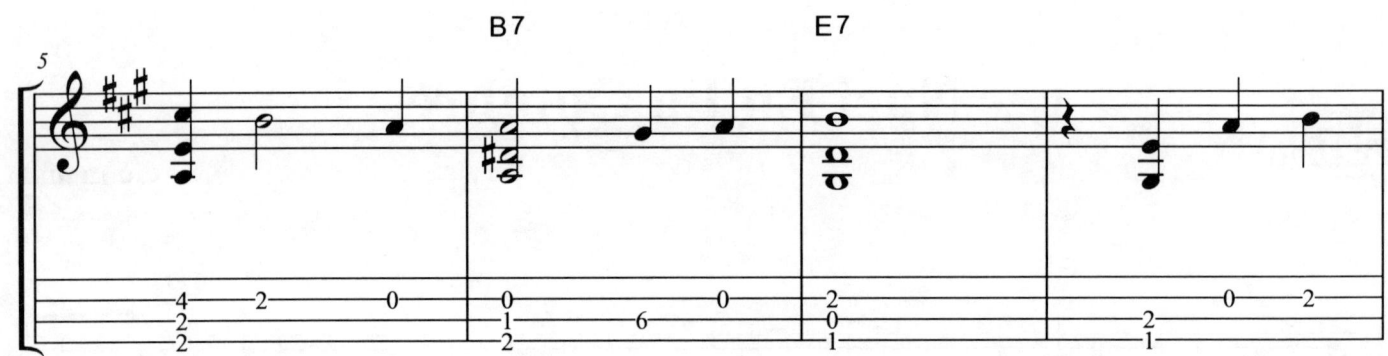
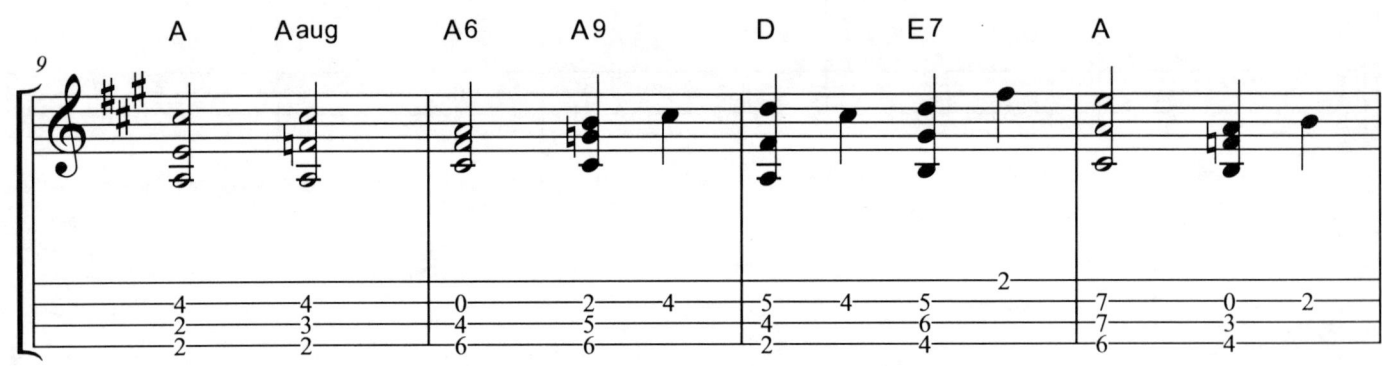
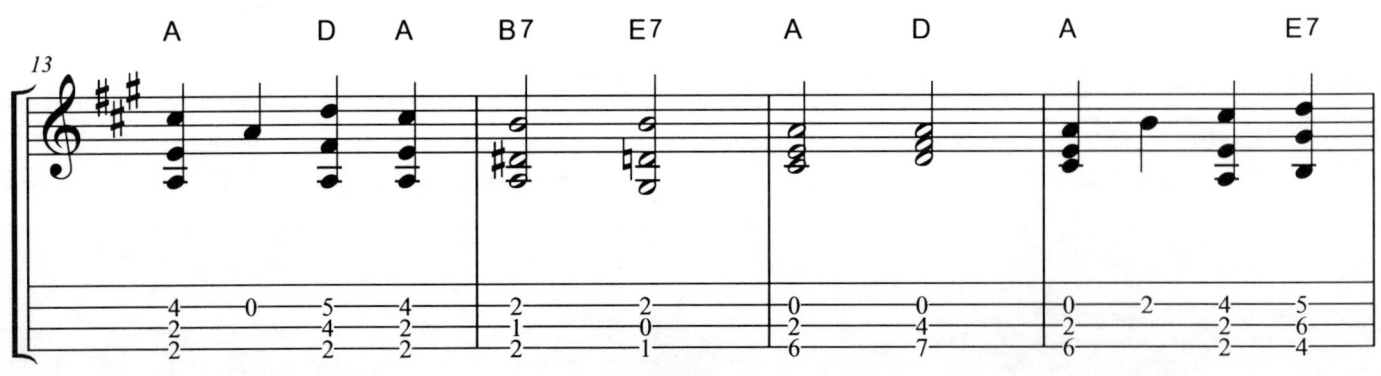

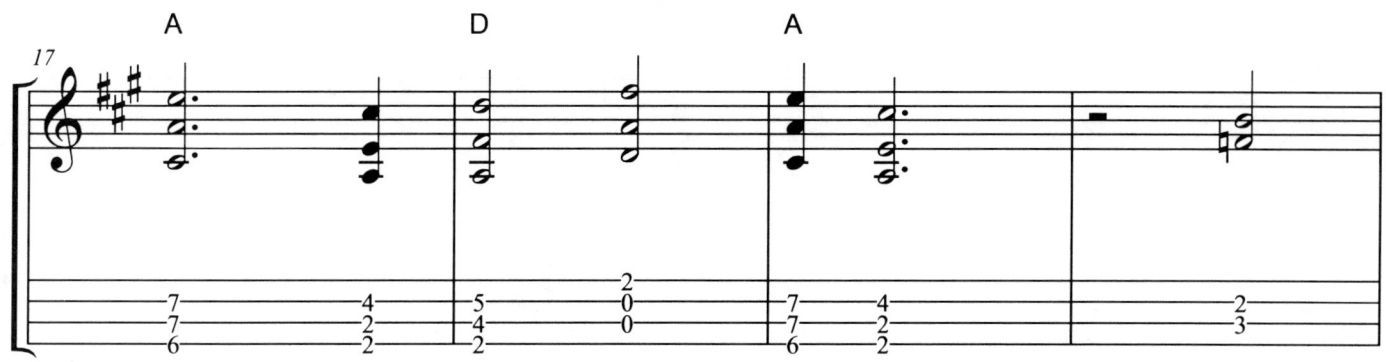
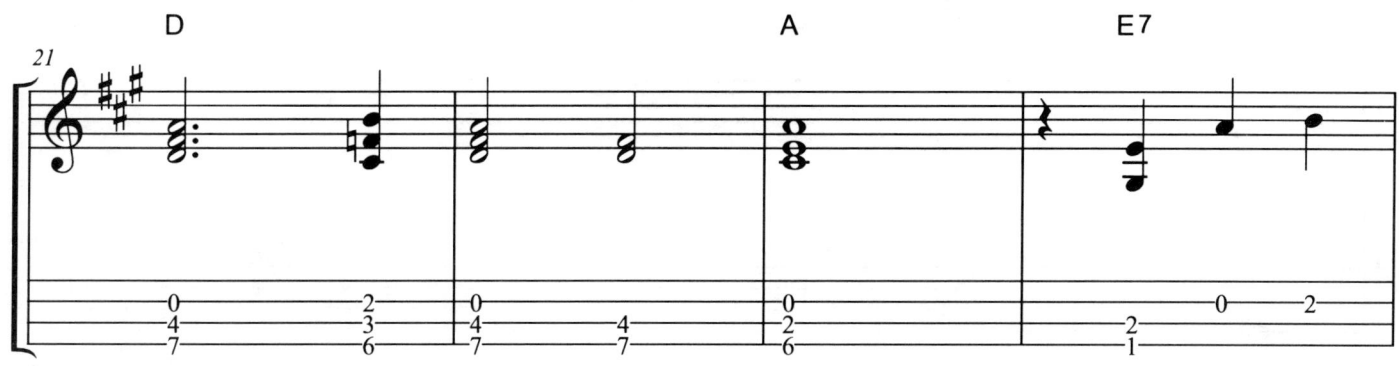
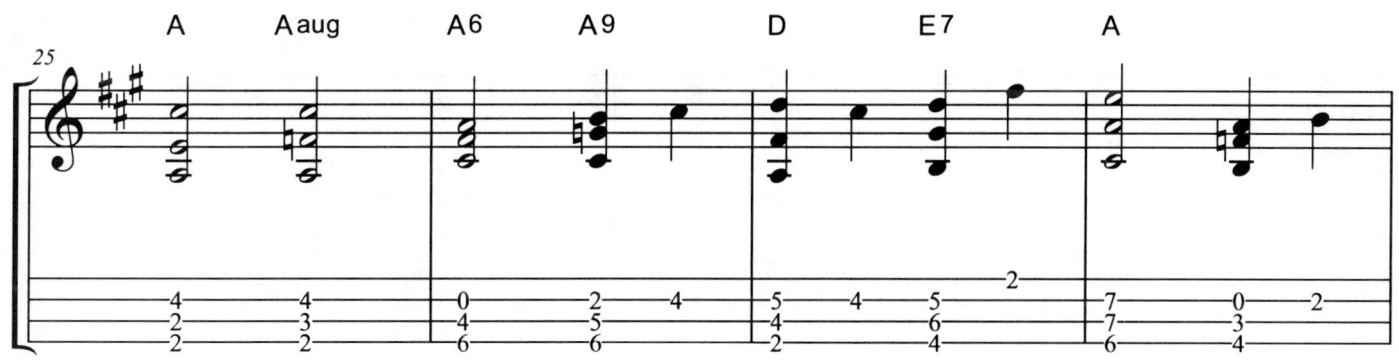
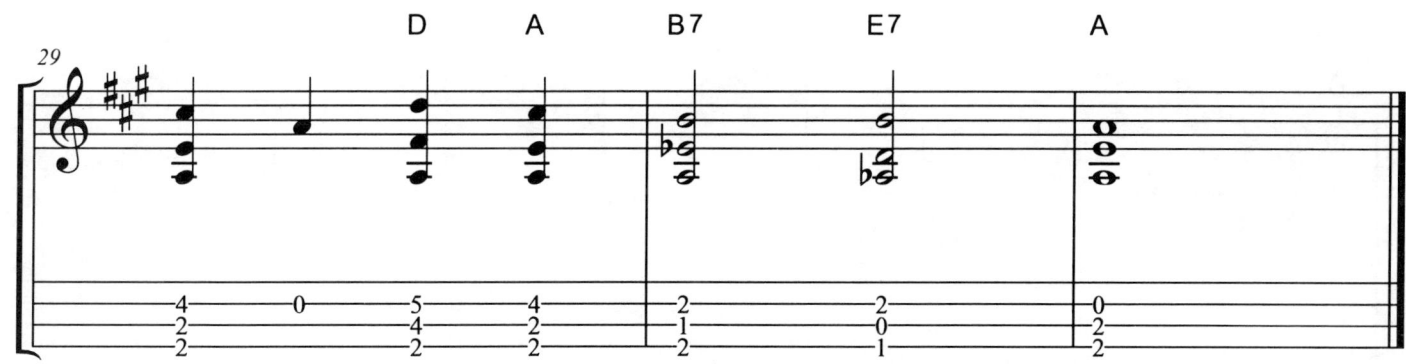

# Herr Roloff's Farewell

**J. Scott Skinner - Scotland**

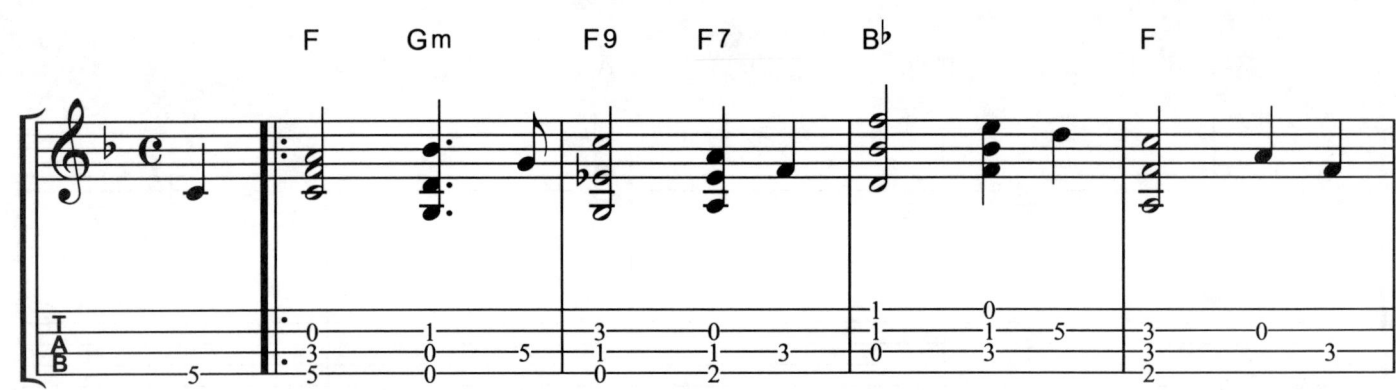
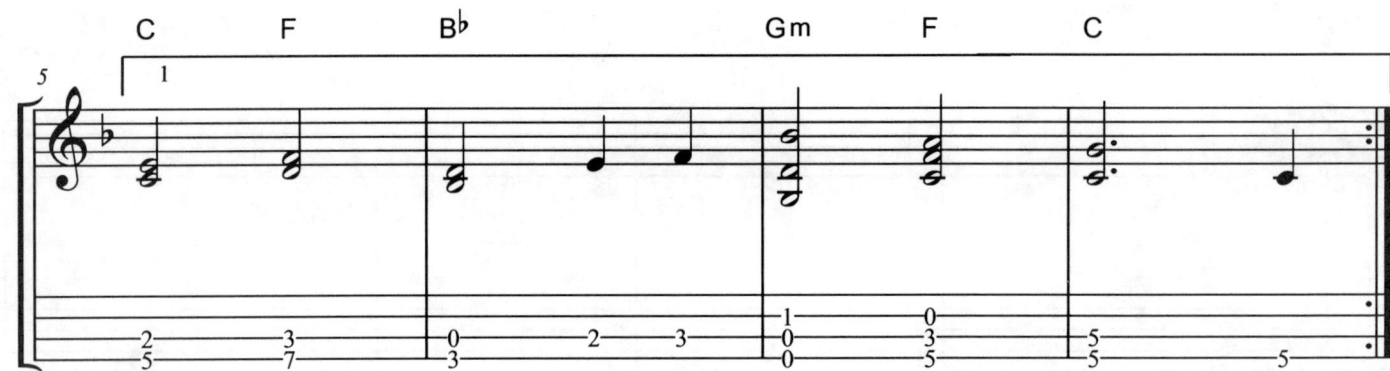
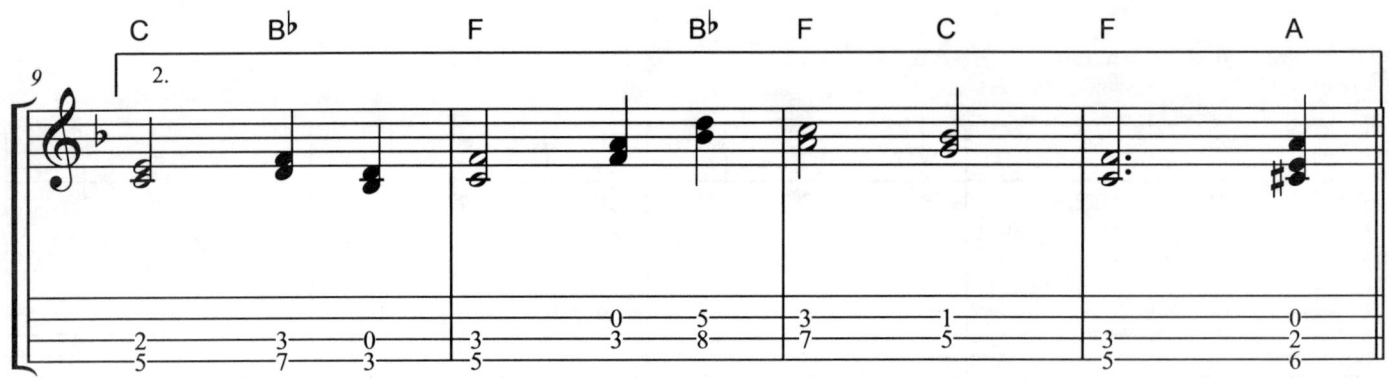
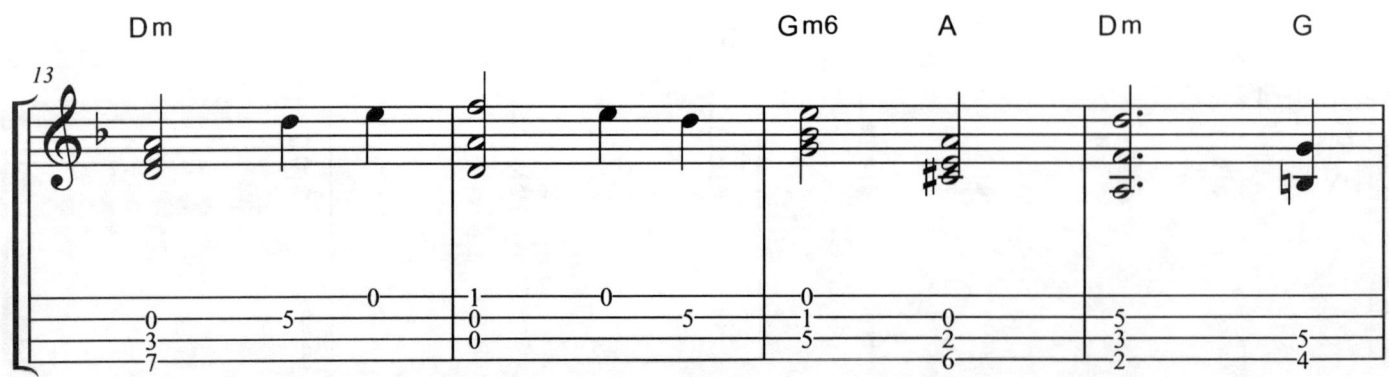

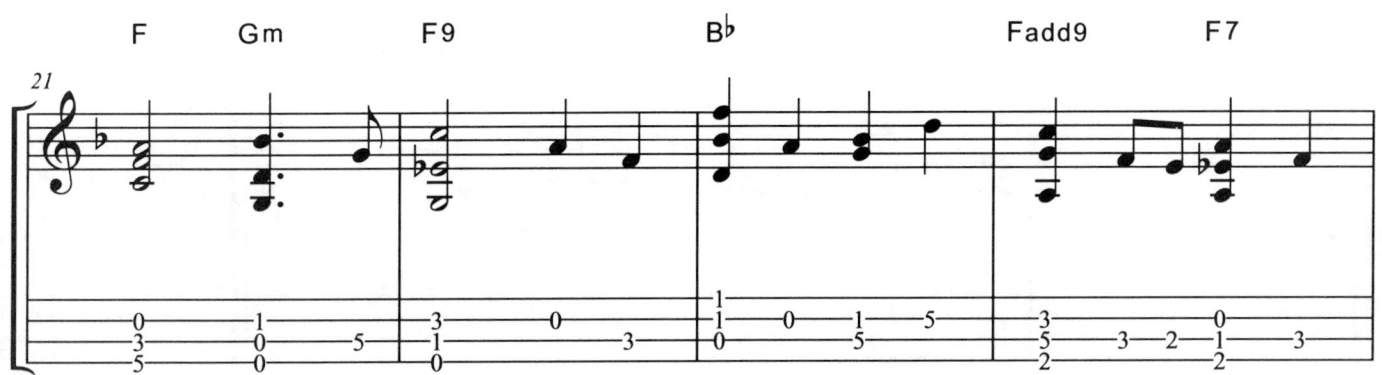

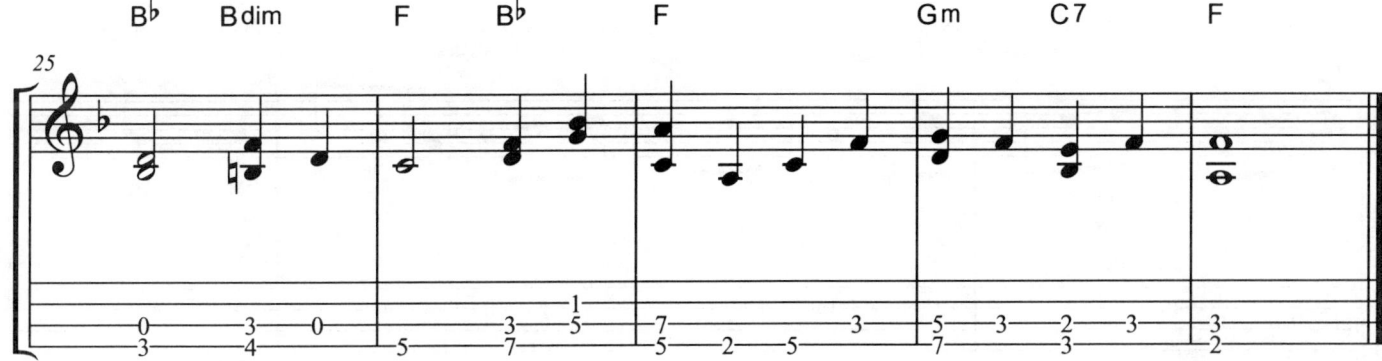

# Tarantella

Italy

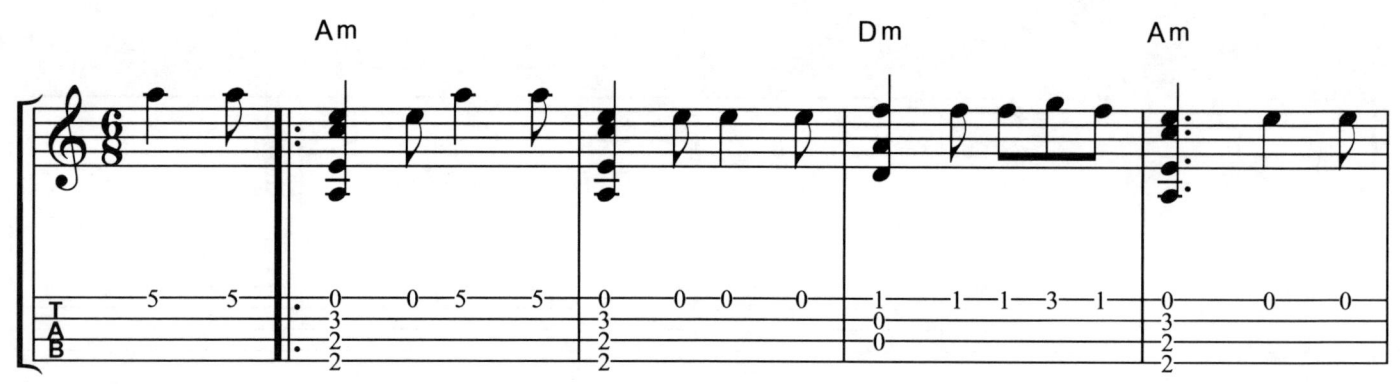

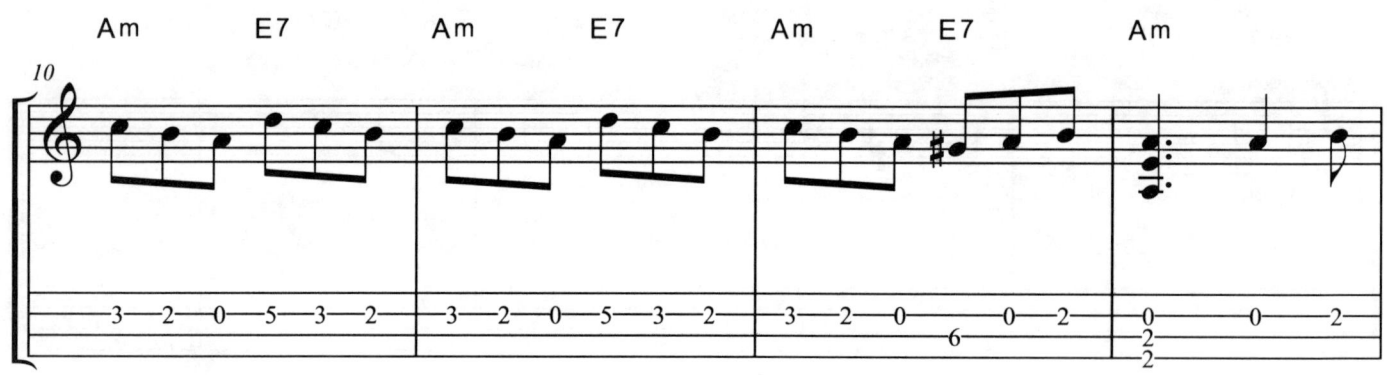
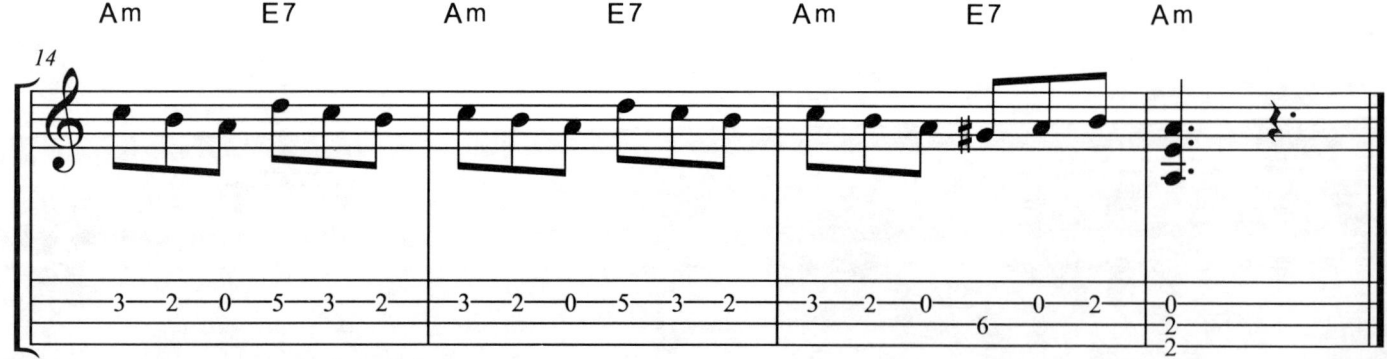

# Volga Boatman

Russia

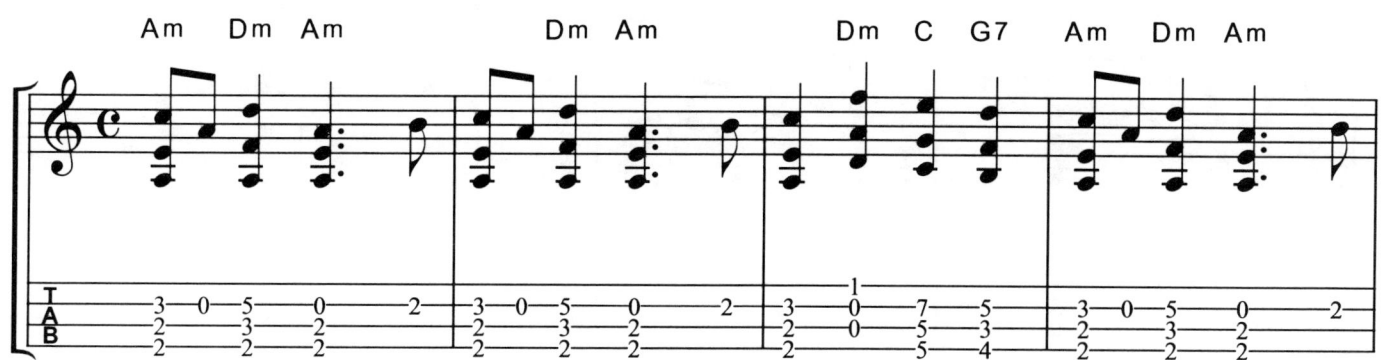
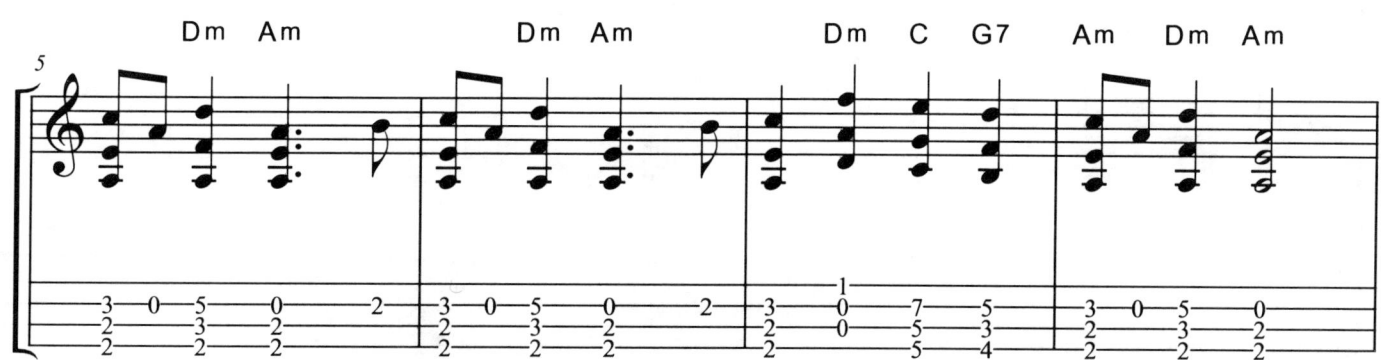
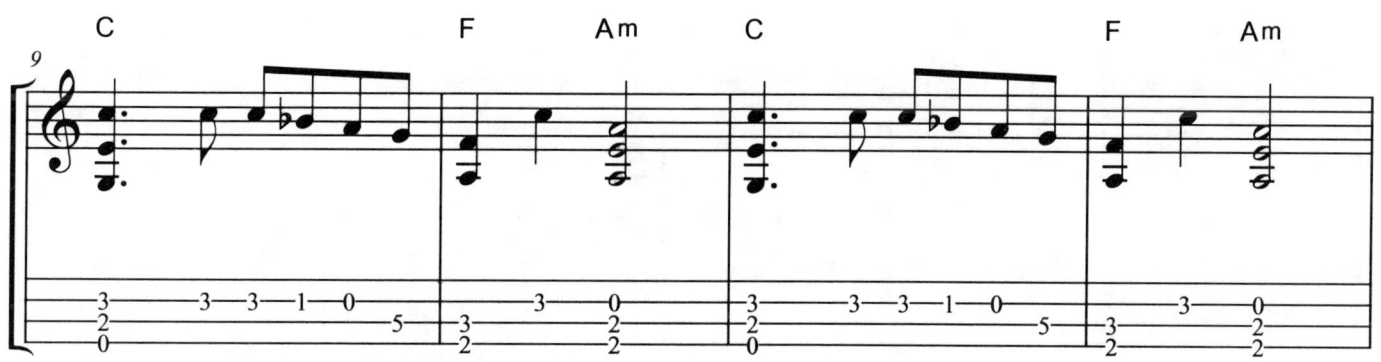
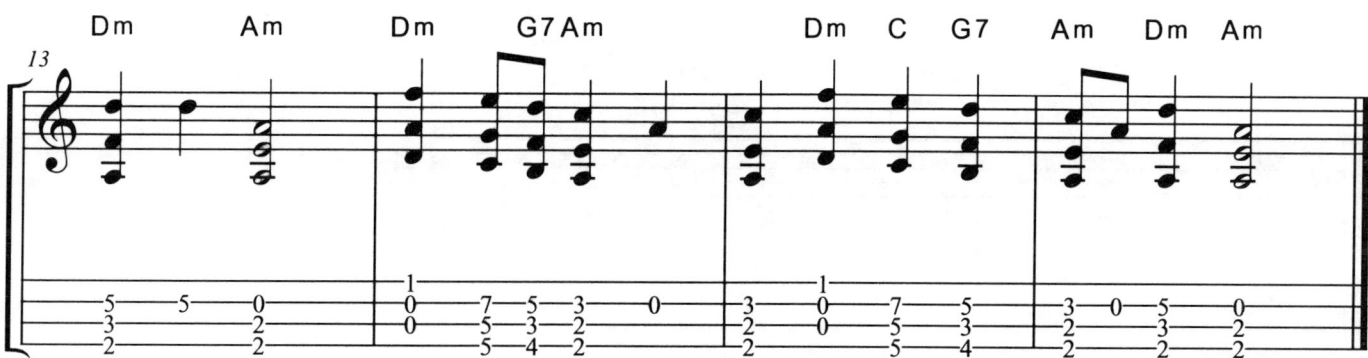

# Waltzing Matilda

Australia

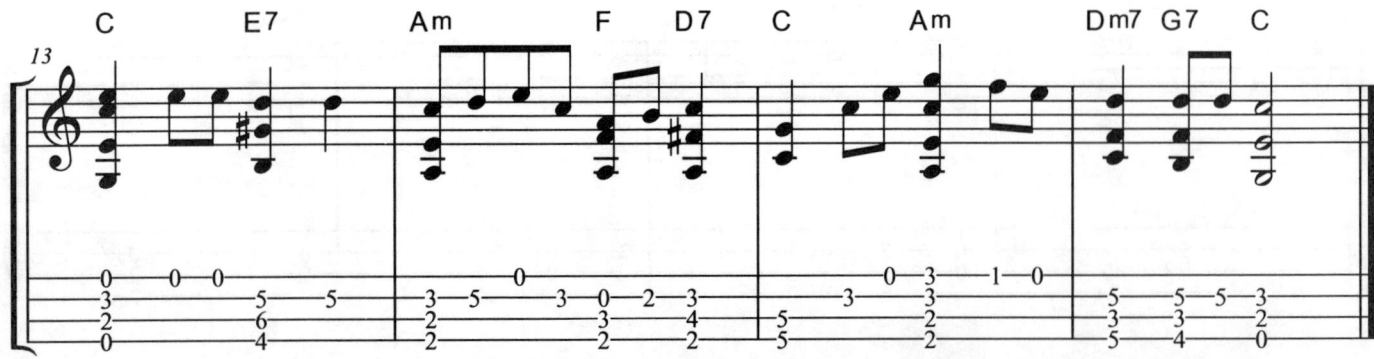

# Riu Chiu (Guardo El Lobo)

Spain

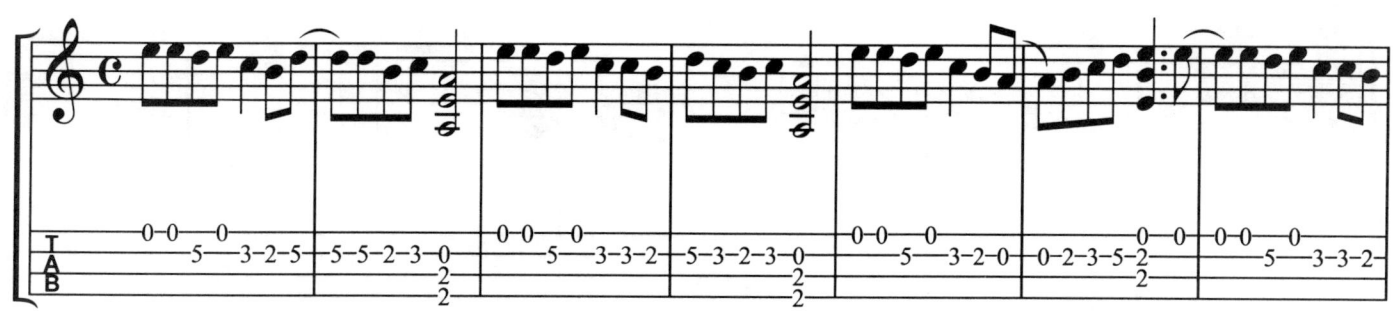

# Sakura - Cherry Blossom

Japan

# The National Anthem

**United States**

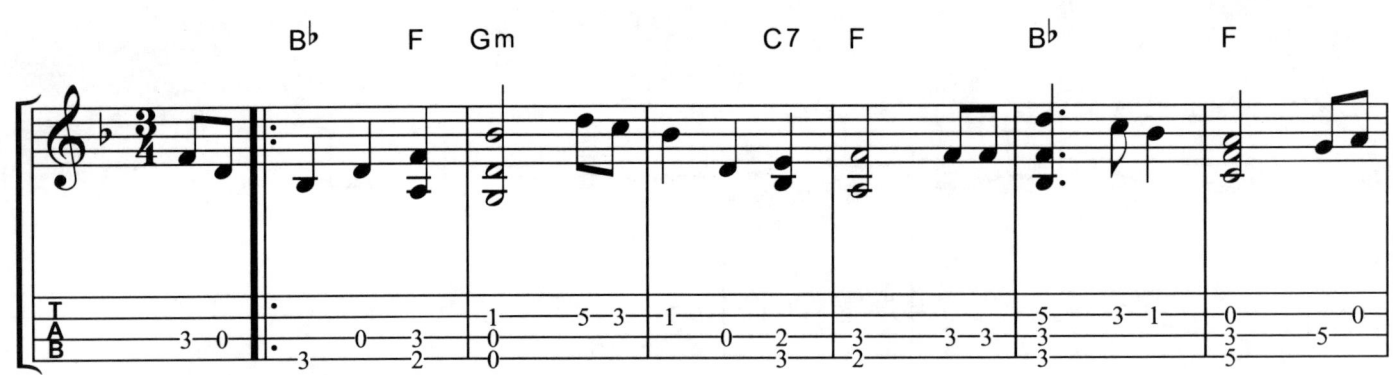
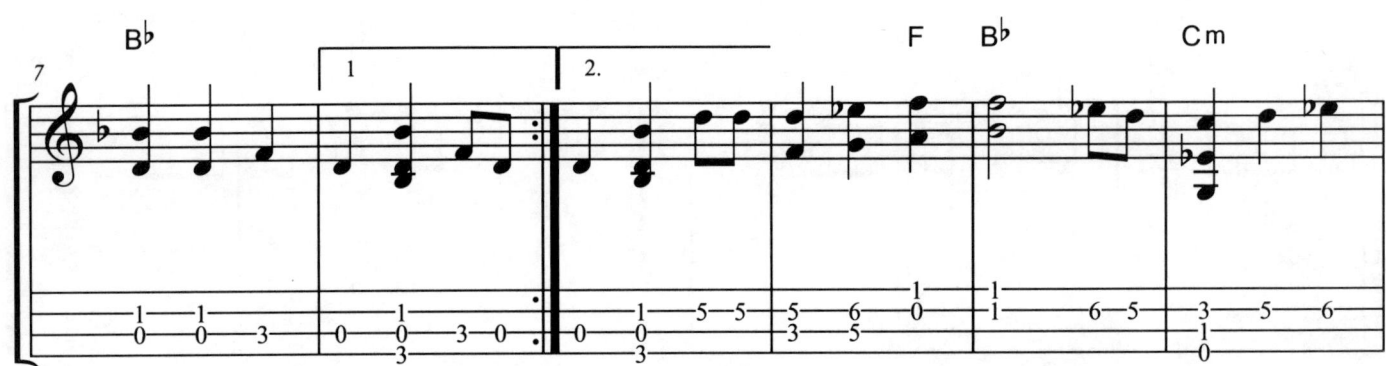
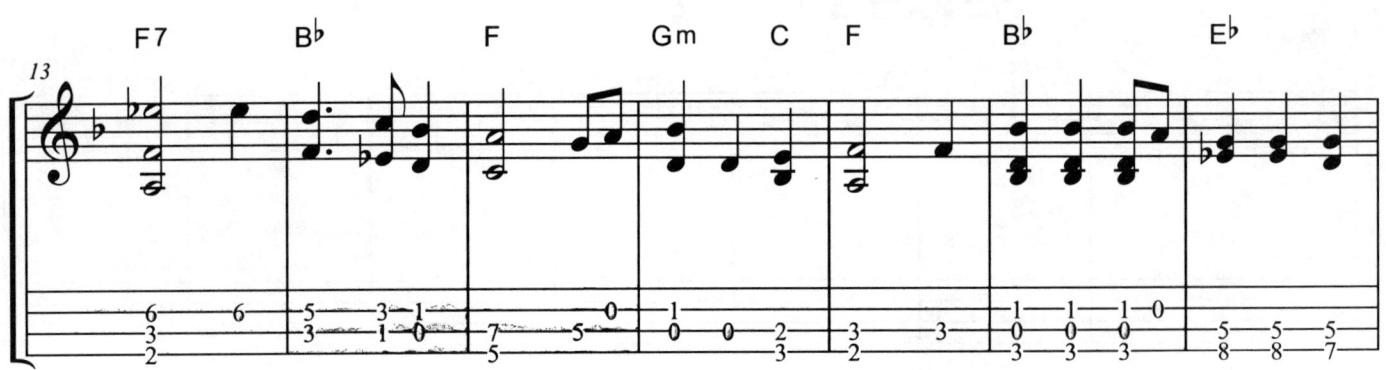
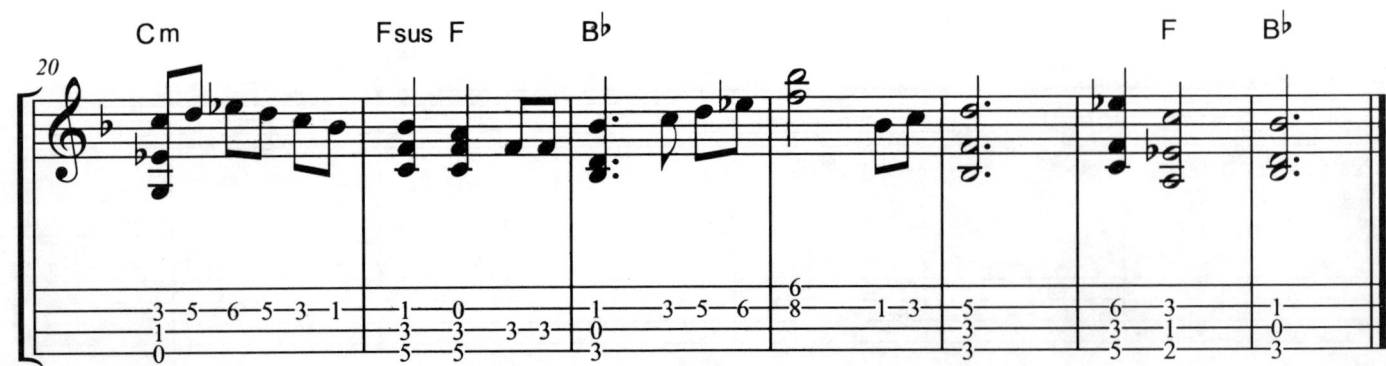